THE FAITH NEX

THE FAITH NEXT DOOR

*American Christians
and Their New
Religious Neighbors*

PAUL D. NUMRICH

OXFORD
UNIVERSITY PRESS

2009

OXFORD
UNIVERSITY PRESS

Oxford University Press, Inc., publishes works that further
Oxford University's objective of excellence
in research, scholarship, and education.

Oxford   New York
Auckland   Cape Town   Dar es Salaam   Hong Kong   Karachi
Kuala Lumpur   Madrid   Melbourne   Mexico City   Nairobi
New Delhi   Shanghai   Taipei   Toronto

With offices in
Argentina   Austria   Brazil   Chile   Czech Republic   France   Greece
Guatemala   Hungary   Italy   Japan   Poland   Portugal   Singapore
South Korea   Switzerland   Thailand   Turkey   Ukraine   Vietnam

Published by Oxford University Press, Inc.
198 Madison Avenue, New York, New York 10016

www.oup.com

Oxford is a registered trademark of Oxford University Press

Library of Congress Cataloging-in-Publication Data

Numrich, Paul David, 1952–
The faith next door : American Christians and their new
religious neighbors / Paul D. Numrich.
    p.   cm.
ISBN 978-0-19-538621-9
1. Christianity and other religions—Illinois—Chicago Region—Case studies.
2. Chicago Region (Ill.)—Religion—Case studies.   I. Title.
BR560.C4N86 2009
261.209773'23—dc22   2008043490

9 8 7 6 5 4 3 2 1

Printed in the United States of America
on acid-free paper

For Christine, of course

Foreword

SINCE THE CHANGES TO U.S. immigration laws in 1965, the American ethnic and religious landscape has shifted dramatically. The truism that the U.S. is "a nation of immigrants" is no longer just a platitude. It has a material impact on the everyday experience and consciousness of most Americans. Walk down the street of any major city, and you are likely to overhear conversations in any one of a number of languages. You may encounter multilingual signage on billboards and in shop windows. The religious streetscape may incorporate not only churches and synagogues, but mosques, temples, gurdwaras, or meditation centers. And, increasingly, you don't need to travel to an urban area to experience such diversity, as smaller cities and towns also host an increasing influx of immigrant populations.

Religious communities are primary locations for such encounters because they are important institutions for forming and maintaining identities, promoting ethics and values that shape civic engagement, and providing a setting for regular social interaction. This is true for both old-timers and newcomers in cities and towns. But religious communities may also create boundaries that make cross-cultural encounters difficult or contentious.

Until recently, little information has been available for understanding these trends or for comprehending the role that faith communities might play in the process. Sociologists and political scientists studying immigration paid very little attention to the religious lives of new immigrants and focused instead on their political and economic characteristics. Historians mostly addressed much earlier immigration periods, which raises the question of how post-1965 changes might be similar to or different from, say, the changes in the late nineteenth century. Theologians had things to say about the relationship of the Christian faith to other faiths, as well as the competing truth claims of various religions, but concentrated less on the practical empirical experience of interfaith encounters. Where was a body to turn?

Paul Numrich has stepped into this gap and provides some important resources for individuals and faith communities struggling with how to responsibly engage human and religious diversity in their local contexts. He draws on the burgeoning new scholarship on religion and immigration, both in social scientific and historical research. He also engages the theological traditions of American faith communities. But more important, he shows us how a variety of such communities are actually answering these difficult cross-cultural and interfaith questions in their real-world, on-the-ground activities and worship lives.

I was fortunate to have a front-row seat as Numrich and his research assistants scattered across the Chicago metro region to spend time with a broad range of Christian congregations, trying to discover how they were actually engaging religious "others." They attended services and potluck dinners, interviewed church leaders, and spoke with parishioners. I can vouch for the meticulous and careful work they did in gathering and analyzing their observations and data. However, unlike in the standard scholarly models, Numrich does not simply provide a set of findings, a few neat answers that readers are expected to accept because they trust his scholarly expertise. Instead, he provides readers with examples, case studies of the rich variety of ways that Christian communities are dealing with new and sometimes strange religious neighbors. Moreover, he draws on his and others' careful scholarship to provide concepts, tools, and leading questions that allow readers to struggle with these issues for themselves and to develop their own strategies for encountering others civilly, responsibly, even lovingly. In doing so, he offers a valuable gift to American citizens of faith and their congregations—a gift that, properly used, will enhance the local religious and civic life of American communities.

Fred Kniss
Professor of Sociology
Loyola University Chicago

Acknowledgments

THIS BOOK WAS MADE POSSIBLE primarily by a grant from the Louisville Institute, whose mission is "to enrich the religious life of American Christians and to encourage the revitalization of their institutions, by bringing together those who lead religious institutions with those who study them, so that the work of each might stimulate and inform the other" (http://www. louisville-institute.org). My special thanks go to Executive Director James W. Lewis for his support and advice throughout the project. Supplemental funding was secured from the Pluralism Project of Harvard University and the Center for the Advanced Study of Christianity and Culture, Loyola University Chicago. My additional thanks go to Fr. Michael Perko, S.J., director of the Center for the Advanced Study of Christianity and Culture; Dr. Randal Hepner of the Religion, Immigration, and Civil Society in Chicago Project, Loyola University; Dr. David Daniels, Dr. Elfriede Wedam, and the late Dr. Lowell Livezey, my colleagues in the Religion in Urban America Program at the University of Illinois at Chicago, for their valuable insights on the project; Dr. R. Stephen Warner, recently retired from the Sociology Department of the University of Illinois at Chicago, for his long-standing encouragement of my research on American religious diversity; and Cynthia Read, Justin Tackett, Paul Hobson, and two anonymous reviewers of Oxford University Press for their encouragement and critical acumen.

From 2002 to 2004 several graduate students from the Sociology and Anthropology Department of Loyola University ably assisted me in the initial research for this book: Suzanne Bundy, Nori Henk, Saher Selod, and Sarah Schott. Along the way they also developed their own scholarly interests in the project. With the approval of Loyola's Institutional Review Board for the Protection of Human Subjects, we conducted semistructured interviews and field observations in the Chicago area after choosing research sites and subjects for their illustrative suitability for the book. We also incorporated data from the Religion, Immigration, and Civil Society in Chicago Project, Loyola University, particularly field research by graduate students Kersten Bayt Priest and Matthew Logelin. Principals from the case studies in the book reviewed draft versions of their chapters in order to fact-check the information and offer feedback on the presentation. In addition, Dr. Fred Kniss, Director of the McNamara Center for the Social Study of Religion, Loyola University, where this project was housed, contributed his expertise, encouragement, and collegiality to this endeavor. My colleagues and students at the Theological Consortium of Greater Columbus, along with churches and other interested groups that invited me to report my findings, were supportive of the premise of this book from the day I arrived in central Ohio. Not only did they help me to fine-tune it, but they also convinced me that these case studies illuminate important national dynamics (see introduction). Finally, my eternal gratitude goes to the many good people whose stories and perspectives grace the pages of this book. They hold the key to the future of our multireligious America.

Contents

THE FAITH NEXT DOOR

Introduction: America's New Religious Diversity

THE PLACE: THE GRAND OLD Palmer House hotel in downtown Chicago. The year: 1993. The event: the Parliament of the World's Religions, a gathering of some eight thousand representatives of the religions of the world on the centennial of the historic World's Parliament of Religions, also held in Chicago. The objectives (among others): "promote understanding and cooperation among religious communities and institutions" and "encourage the spirit of harmony and to celebrate, with openness and mutual respect, the rich diversity of religions."

As a historian of religions, I knew the significance of the first parliament in 1893, which many mark as the beginning of the modern interfaith dialogue movement. I attended this second parliament partly out of scholarly curiosity but also as an ordained Christian minister interested in the implications of such dramatic, multireligious conclaves for local Christians. When the religions of the world "come to town," so to speak, how do Christians respond?

Actually, the 1993 parliament raised an even more pressing question: How do local Christians respond when they discover that the religions of the world now reside in their town? Most of the non-Christian representatives to the first parliament came to Chicago from other countries. The organizers of the 1993 parliament invited the religious communities of Chicago to form host committees for the event, more than half of which turned out to be non-Christian: Baha'i, Buddhist, Hindu, Jain, Jewish, Muslim, Sikh, and Zoroastrian. Christian host committees were formed by the local Anglican, Orthodox, Protestant, and Roman Catholic communities. Thus, Chicago in the 1990s was a multireligious metropolis, and many local Christians welcomed the new diversity as an opportunity for mutual celebration and understanding.

Many, but by no means all. If the 1993 parliament was any indication, Chicago-area Christians varied significantly in their responses to the new religious diversity in their midst. Outside the Palmer House, a group condemned the parliament for supporting idolatry on American soil in violation of this nation's sacred covenant with Almighty God. Several evangelical Christian groups chose not to attend the parliament, and some that did expressed reservations about it. For instance, Pastor Erwin Lutzer of Chicago's famous Moody Church complained that the proceedings privileged non-Christian faiths: "Jesus did not get a fair representation here," he told the *Chicago Tribune*. A few days into the eight-day event, the Orthodox Christian delegation withdrew in protest over the presence of groups "which profess no belief in God or a supreme being" and "certain quasi-religious groups with which Orthodox Christians share no common ground." Media reports suggested Buddhism, Hinduism, and neopaganism as the most likely causes for offense to Orthodox sensibilities.

Much of the Christian criticism of the 1993 parliament hinged on the implied equivalency of the religious truth claims of the various participants. For instance, the Tzemach Institute of Biblical Studies, a ministry of Fellowship Church in Casselberry, Florida, features the parliament in an article that rejects the notion that Christianity can live in harmony with any "religion," defined here as a false belief system that does not recognize the unique authority of Jesus and the Bible. Likewise, Apologetics Index, an evangelical Web site that provides resources on "religious movements, cults, sects, world religions, and related issues," lists the parliament's organizing body, the Council for a Parliament of the World's Religions, as an organization that promotes "religious pluralism," which the Apologetics Index defines as the theory that "more than one religion can be said to have the truth...even if their essential doctrines are mutually exclusive" and rejects as inconsistent with Christian evangelism. Notable denominations with similar views about competing religious truth claims include the Southern Baptist Convention, the nation's largest

SIDEBAR I.1
Excerpt from "Resolution On The Finality Of Jesus Christ As Sole And Sufficient Savior," Southern Baptist Convention

...WHEREAS, Christianity is often presented in the context of world religions as merely one of the many expressions of humanity's religious consciousness, all of which are seen as independently valid ways of knowing God; and
WHEREAS, Theological accommodation in this critical area of faith and doctrine seriously compromises our evangelistic witness and missionary outreach to the lost....

Be it...RESOLVED, That we oppose the false teaching that Christ is so evident in world religions, human consciousness or the natural process that one can encounter Him and find salvation without the direct means of the gospel, or that adherents of the non-Christian religions and world views can receive this salvation through any means other than personal repentance and faith in Jesus Christ, the only Savior....

Source: http://www.sbc.net/resolutions/amResolution.asp?ID=651.

Protestant denomination, and the Assemblies of God, the nation's largest Pentecostal denomination (see sidebars I.1 and I.2). The issue of religious truth claims resurfaces throughout this book.

A decade after the 1993 Parliament of the World's Religions, non-Christian religious communities claimed large numbers of adherents in the Chicago metropolitan area: 2,000 Baha'is, 150,000 Buddhists, 80,000 Hindus, 7,000 Jains, 260,000 Jews, 400,000 Muslims, 6,000 Sikhs, and 700 Zoroastrians. Some of these figures, published in 2004 by the local branch of the National Conference for Community and Justice (formerly the National Conference of Christians and Jews), may be inflated (self-estimates are always suspect, no matter what the group). But Chicago's growing religious diversity cannot be denied.

SIDEBAR I.2
Excerpt from "Non-Christian Religions,"
Assemblies of God

Why doesn't the Assemblies of God accept non-Christian religions as valid means of salvation and access to God?...The
Bible is clear in its insistence on belief in the Lord Jesus Christ
as the only way for sinners to get right with God and to be ready
for heaven. To tolerate non-Christian alternative views is to
deny to masses of people the only way of salvation, for without
Christ they will perish....In our day, there is a steady drumbeat
of support for toleration, as a humane and generous way to live.
The earnest Christian will distinguish between respect and toleration of other human beings as individuals made in the image
of God, whether or not they accept the Christian mandate, as
opposed to toleration of destructive ideas that are hostile to
Christian revelation and society at large. To confuse the issue of
toleration for persons and the toleration of alien ideas is at the
root of the issue.

Source: http://ag.org/top/Beliefs/gendoct_16_religions.cfm.

And Chicago mirrors the nation. The Pluralism Project at
Harvard University has tracked America's growing religious diversity since the early 1990s. In 2008 the project's Web site posted
the figures shown in table I.1. America's new religious landscape
is not confined to major metropolises like Chicago. The Pluralism
Project has researched religious diversity in Maine, Mississippi,
Kansas, the Miami Valley in Ohio, Phoenix, and numerous other
areas across the country.

Of course, national estimates may also be inflated, particularly
self-estimates of adherents. That granted, even critics of commonly
reported figures like those in the middle column of table 1.1 admit
that the United States is more religiously diverse today than ever
before and will likely continue to diversify in the future. However,
debates over *quantitative* measures of America's non-Christian

TABLE I.1.: Selected Non-Christian Religions in the United States, 2008

Religion	Adherents	Centers/Groups
Baha'i	142,245–753,000	1,152
Buddhism	2,450,000–4,000,000	2,203
Hinduism	1,200,000	711
Islam	2,560,000–6,000,000	1,646
Jainism	25,000–75,000	69
Judaism	5,621,000–6,150,000	NA
Sikhism	250,000	252

Source: Pluralism Project, http://www.pluralism.org/resources/statistics/ tradition.php.

population miss the point of the crucial *qualitative* shift in its self-perception as a religious nation in recent years. Although still a predominantly Christian country in terms of the religious self-identity of its residents, the United States increasingly perceives itself as a multireligious society, and this shift holds no matter what one thinks of the new religious diversity. Locally this change can occur when a single mosque, temple, or other non-Christian religious center joins a previously all-Christian landscape. Indeed, most of the interviewees for this book were vague on the names and identities of the non-Christian centers in their vicinities, yet they were quite aware of the new religious presence around them. A perceptual modification can also occur as the result of media reports and features on diverse American religious groups.

How did the United States reach its present level of multireligious diversity? It is almost cliché today to tout the cultural significance of the 1960s, but to answer this question we correctly look to the ferment of that decade. Two major social trends that either began or intensified in the 1960s have significantly diversified the American religious landscape in the early twenty-first century.

First, steadily increasing numbers of immigrants entered the United States after the changes in U.S. immigration law that began in 1965. Restrictive immigration policies that had been in place since the 1920s were relaxed, and historic preferences for European immigrants set aside. From the 1950s to the 1990s, European immigration dropped from 53 percent of the total immigrant flow to a mere 15 percent, while Latin American and Asian

immigration increased from 31 percent to a substantial 78 percent
of the total. The Asian increase accounted for most of the growth
in America's non-Christian population, particularly in the numbers of the three largest non-Christian groups: Muslims (mostly
from the Middle East and South Asia), Buddhists (mostly from
East and Southeast Asia), and Hindus (from India and countries
with secondary Indian settlement).

The second major social trend affecting America's religious
landscape did not strictly begin in the 1960s but certainly intensified in that decade and beyond. This involved significant numbers
raised in America's historically mainstream religions of Christianity
and Judaism who converted to "alternative" or "new" religions or
at least were influenced by them to a notable degree. The roots of
this conversion/influence trend can be traced to earlier decades,
especially the so-called Zen boom among white Americans in the
1950s and the so-called Black Muslim movement among African
Americans, which began in the 1930s. Even so, the 1960s ushered
in a new era of spiritual inquisitiveness in the indigenous population that, when combined with the new immigration, has created
today's multireligious America.

Figures I.1 and I.2 provide selected indicators of the recent
growth in America's non-Christian religions. The first shows the
number of Muslim mosques, both immigrant and convert, established in the United States in each decade since the 1920s (from a
sample total of 416 mosques). The second figure shows the number of Buddhist meditation centers established in North America
between 1900 and 1997 (from a sample total of 1,062 centers,
mostly of the convert type). In both cases the increase since the
1960s is dramatic. Even if recent trends in immigration and spiritual inquisitiveness have crested, their sustained effects on U.S.
society are substantial.

In his 1983 book, *Christians and Religious Pluralism,* theologian Alan Race argues that the modern age has forced a dilemma
on Christians, that of evaluating "the relationship between the
Christian faith and the faith of the other religions." Race identifies several factors that contribute to this dilemma, including
new knowledge from the academic study of world religions and
increasing personal contacts with adherents of other faiths. After

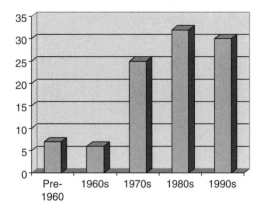

FIGURE I.1. Percentage of U.S. Muslim Mosques by Decade of Establishment. Source: Ihsan Bagby, Paul M. Perl, and Bryan T. Froehle, *The Mosque in America: A National Portrait* (Washington, D.C.: Council on American-Islamic Relations, 2001).

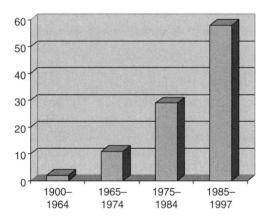

FIGURE I.2. Percentage of U.S. Buddhist Meditation Centers by Period of Establishment. Source: Don Morreale, *The Complete Guide to Buddhist America* (Boston: Shambhala, 1998).

noting in their 1996 volume, *Ministry and Theology in Global Perspective,* that Christians disagree among themselves "on virtually every issue of substance," Don Pittman, Ruben Habito, and Terry Muck make this further point: "Among the defining practical theological issues of our time that are surrounded by debate,

perhaps none poses a more difficult set of interrelated founda-
tional questions than the relation of Christians to people of other
living faiths and ideologies." These authors also cite a memorable
quip by comparative religion scholar Wilfred Cantwell Smith that
epitomizes the modern Christian dilemma: "We explain the fact
that the Milky Way is there by the doctrine of creation, but how
do we explain the fact that the Bhagavad Gita [a Hindu scripture]
is there?"

Christians can choose to avoid such theological questions posed
by the living non-Christian religions, and Christian congregations
can choose to ignore the non-Christians living and worshiping in
their neighborhoods. However, if Christians make such choices,
they should realize that these, too, are responses to religious diversity. We do not have the option of doing "nothing" since even avoidance is doing something. The Christian congregations and groups
described in this book have responded to religious diversity out of
deliberate conviction. Their choices are meant to prompt you to
act with the same level of deliberate conviction, no matter what
choices you make.

About This Book

The idea for this book grew slowly during my years of
researching America's new religious diversity. I watched with
interest the media coverage of the topic, such as the CBS News
documentary, *The Strangers Next Door,* about "trialogues" among
Jews, Christians, and Muslims organized by the Greater Detroit
Interfaith Roundtable in response to a proposed mosque in
Bloomfield Hills, Michigan. I read articles like Terry Muck's essay
in the evangelical periodical *Christianity Today,* titled "The Mosque
Next Door: How Do We Speak the Truth in Love to Muslims,
Hindus, and Buddhists?" I noted projects like "The Sikh Next
Door: Introducing Sikhs to America's Classrooms," which provides
educational materials for sixth and seventh graders, funded by the
September 11th Anti-Bias Project of the National Conference for
Community and Justice. In addition, I accepted invitations from
local church groups to help them understand their new religious

neighbors, whether they were Muslims, Hindus, Buddhists, Sikhs, or groups only vaguely known.

It finally dawned on me to turn the focus around in order to examine what is happening in Christian groups and congregations in religiously diverse settings in the United States. How are they relating to the new "faith next door," that is, to the new mosques, temples, and other non-Christian religious centers of America? Here are on-the-ground case studies of the issues, challenges, and decision-making dynamics involved in local Christian responses to the nation's new multireligious reality. This book will appeal to Christian readers at all points on the theological spectrum and from all denominational (or nondenominational) backgrounds who wish to learn from Christians who have squarely faced the realities of America's growing religious diversity and, in the process, have discovered effective and satisfactory ways of defining their own Christian identity and mission. This book offers a broad, balanced, and sympathetic sampling of the variety of local Christian responses so that readers can make informed decisions about their own stances vis-à-vis their non-Christian neighbors. It will also inform non-Christian readers and general observers about important trends in American Christianity.

The book features eleven case-study chapters of local Christian congregations and groups—Protestants, Catholics, and Orthodox; conservatives and liberals; native born and foreign born; whites and African Americans. Several chapters are paired topically and can be studied together to good effect: Chapters 2 and 3 on evangelicals, chapters 4 and 5 on different approaches to Islam, chapters 7 and 8 on Catholics, and chapters 8 and 9 on African American Christians and Muslims. The ordering of the chapters does not imply any kind of theological trend since the remarkable variety of Christian perspectives on other religions is as evident today as it was in the mid-1980s, when the first Hindu temple was built in Aurora, Illinois (chapter 1). However, the lack of public response to the opening of Aurora's second Hindu temple, as well as the fact that most of the churches involved in the initial controversy have not pursued the issue of religious diversity in any systematic way (chapter 11), may indicate a growing willingness among Christians to grant civic accommodation to America's increasing religious variety. For some, this may mean nothing more than resignation to demographic realities.

The case-study chapters are bracketed by introductory and concluding chapters on the nation's new religious diversity and the implications for Christians. The format of the book fits a typical congregational adult or young adult education unit, covering one or two chapters per week, but the book can also be used for individual study. Each chapter includes a section titled "For More Information," which expands on key topics and identifies resources for further investigation. Since this book is not primarily about non-Christian religious groups and centers but rather about Christians' responses to them, readers interested in exploring the beliefs and practices of America's new religions will find resources in the "For More Information" sections. Each chapter ends with a set of questions and Bible passages titled "For Discussion," designed to stimulate further thought about important points.

Chapters have been kept to a manageable length in order to encourage substantive exploration and reflection on topics of interest to readers. Although this book is based on scholarly research, it is written without academic jargon and the usual scholarly accoutrements, such as footnotes or a conventional bibliography. Information about source materials can be found in the "For More Information" sections of the chapters (all Web sites were functional as of July 2008). Group study leaders may wish to assign specific tasks to individuals in preparation for upcoming sessions, such as consulting the resources listed under "For More Information."

The combination of local context, practical theology, breadth of perspective, and suitability for group study distinguishes this book from others on the topic of Christianity and other religions. Here Christian theology meets the multireligious real world of contemporary America—with multiple results. The case studies featured in this book are suggestive of national trends. To be sure, locale matters in the relationships between Christians and their new non-Christian neighbors, but the Chicago lens of this book illuminates dynamics at work across a multireligious America. I encourage readers to consider the implications for the faiths next door to each other in your neighborhood.

For More Information

The Council for a Parliament of the World's Religions can be contacted at 70 E. Lake Street, Suite 205, Chicago, IL 60601, phone 312-629-2990, http://www.parliamentofreligions.org. The council has organized a series of international interfaith parliaments: Chicago (1993), Cape Town (1999), Barcelona (2004), and Melbourne (2009). On the 1993 Parliament in Chicago see Wayne Teasdale and George F. Cairns, eds., *Community of Religion: Voices and Images of the Parliament of the World's Religions* (New York: Continuum, 2000), and the video documentary *Peace like a River,* available from the Chicago Sunday Evening Club, 200 N. Michigan Avenue, Suite 403, Chicago IL 60601, phone 312-236-4483. On the 1893 World's Parliament of Religions see Richard Hughes Seager, *The Dawn of Religious Pluralism: Voices from the World's Parliament of Religions, 1893* (LaSalle, Ill.: Open Court, 1993).

Christian criticisms of the 1993 parliament and of the notion that all religions contain equally valid truth claims can be found at the following Web sites: http://www.tzemach.org/articles/relharm.htm (Tzemach Institute for Biblical Studies, "Religious Harmony?"); http://www.apologeticsindex.org/c54.html (Apologetics Index); http://www.sbc.net/resolutions/amResolution.asp?ID=651 (Southern Baptist Convention, "Resolution on the Finality of Jesus Christ as Sole and Sufficient Savior"); and http://ag.org/top/Beliefs/gendoct_16_religions.cfm (Assemblies of God, "Non-Christian Religions").

The National Conference for Community and Justice (NCCJ) has once again changed its name and now calls itself the Chicago Center for Cultural Connections. Its contact information is 27 E. Monroe Street, Suite 400, Chicago, IL 60603; phone, 312-236-9272; http://www.connections-chicago.org. The September 11th Anti-Bias Project was a joint initiative of the NCCJ and the ChevronTexaco Foundation; see http://www.chevron.com/GlobalIssues/CorporateResponsibility/2003/community_engagement.asp.

The Web site of the Pluralism Project, Harvard University, is http://
www.pluralism.org. The Pluralism Project tracks America's growing religious diversity and promotes a pluralist approach, which
it defines as an active, appreciative, and respectful interchange
among various religious elements of society. For the statistics on
selected world religions in the United States shown in table I.1,
see http://www.pluralism.org/resources/statistics/tradition.php. The
Pluralism Project's Web site also includes information on non-
Christian religious centers across the country and research
initiatives that are mapping America's new religious diversity.

For a study that challenges commonly reported estimates of
America's non-Christian population, see Tom W. Smith, "Religious
Diversity in America: The Emergence of Muslims, Buddhists,
Hindus, and Others," *Journal for the Scientific Study of Religion*
41(3) (September 2002): 577–585.

Readable scholarly treatments of religious trends in the United
States include Robert Wuthnow, *After Heaven: Spirituality in
America since the 1950s* (Berkeley: University of California Press,
1998); Wade Clark Roof, *Spiritual Marketplace: Baby Boomers and
the Remaking of American Religion* (Princeton, N.J.: Princeton
University Press, 2001); and Stephen J. Stein, *Communities of
Dissent: A History of Alternative Religions in America* (New York:
Oxford University Press, 2003). For information on various non-
Christian religions in the United States, see Gurinder Singh Mann,
Paul David Numrich, and Raymond B. Williams, *Buddhists, Hindus,
and Sikhs in America: A Short History* (New York: Oxford University
Press, 2007); Diana L. Eck, *A New Religious America: How a
"Christian Country" Has Now Become the World's Most Religiously
Diverse Nation* (San Francisco: Harper, 2002); Stuart M. Matlins
and Arthur J. Magida, eds., *How to Be a Perfect Stranger: The
Essential Religious Etiquette Handbook,* 4th ed. (Woodstock, Vt.:
SkyLight Paths, 2006); and the Pluralism Project's Web site, http://
www.pluralism.org. Ihsan Bagby, Paul M. Perl, and Bryan T. Froehle,
"The Mosque in America: A National Portrait" (Washington, D.C.:
Council on American-Islamic Relations, 2001), is available from
the Council on American-Islamic Relations, http://www.cair.com/

AmericanMuslims/ReportsandSurveys.aspx. Don Morreale, *The Complete Guide to Buddhist America* (Boston: Shambhala, 1998), focuses primarily on so-called convert Buddhists, that is, those who have adopted Buddhism as their religion of choice rather than having been born Buddhist.

Numerous books address the theological issue of Christianity's relation to other world religions. The two mentioned in the present chapter are Alan Race, *Christians and Religious Pluralism: Patterns in the Christian Theology of Religions* (London: SCM, 1983), and Don A. Pittman, Ruben L. F. Habito, and Terry C. Muck, eds., *Ministry and Theology in Global Perspective: Contemporary Challenges for the Church* (Grand Rapids, Mich.: Eerdmans, 1996). See the conclusion of the present book for more references.

Regarding the 1995 CBS News documentary, *The Strangers Next Door*, contact the National Council of Churches, 475 Riverside Drive, Suite 880, New York, N.Y. 10115, phone 212-870-2228, http://www.ncccusa.org. Terry Muck's essay in *Christianity Today*, "The Mosque Next Door: How Do We Speak the Truth in Love to Muslims, Hindus, and Buddhists?" is discussed in chapter 1 of the present book.

For Discussion

1. Would you or representatives of your congregation have attended the 1993 Parliament of the World's Religions? Why or why not? Which position on the parliament described in this chapter most closely matches your own? What position does your denomination or Christian tradition take on the truth claims of the world's religions?

2. What does it mean that the United States is now a multireligious society? Have you seen evidence of both the *quantitative* increase in non-Christian religions in the United States and the *qualitative* shift in America's religious self-perception?

3. What is the relationship between a religion's truth claims and its size? Christianity is America's (and the world's) largest religion; is that because it is the "truest" religion?

4. Discuss the two major social trends that have significantly diversified America's religious landscape since the 1960s: immigration and spiritual inquisitiveness. Do you know individuals who represent each of these trends? How do you relate to those individuals as a Christian?

5. Having read only this introductory chapter, speculate on what you and/or your congregation might do in response to local religious diversity after completing this book. What are you doing now, and how might that change? If you have done "nothing" until now, was it out of deliberate conviction or for some other reason?

6. Bible passages: Acts 4:12 and 17:29–31 are cited in the Assemblies of God statement, "Non-Christian Religions" (http://ag.org/top/Beliefs/gendoct_16_religions.cfm). Luke 10:25–37, the parable of the Good Samaritan, was featured in a workshop titled "A Christian Approach to Dialogue" at the 1993 Parliament of the World's Religions.

ONE

A Hindu Temple Comes to Town

"AURORA COULD BE HOME FOR the largest Hindu temple in America." Thus began the April 23, 1985, front-page story in the local newspaper informing the residents of Aurora, Illinois, of plans to build a Hindu temple named for Sri Venkateswara, a deity revered in southern India. Four days later, the newspaper's weekly religion section ran an article about Hindu religious practices, with a photo of an Aurora Hindu woman performing *arati*, the ritual waving of an oil lamp, before a small but ornate temporary altar to Sri Venkateswara in the former farmhouse on the proposed temple's property. The article was positioned between regular features about Aurora Christian churches, including a column called "God's Open Window," contributed by Christian clergy. The positioning symbolized the changes about to take place on Aurora's religious landscape.

In the mid-1980s this blue-collar city west of Chicago was home to dozens of churches and a Jewish synagogue. For Aurora, historically populated by European Americans, African Americans, and Hispanics, Indian Hindus represented both a new ethnic presence and an unfamiliar religious tradition. For several months in 1985, Aurora Christians engaged in a public debate about the merits of the proposed Hindu temple, citing both theological and civic positions.

The first letter to the editor of the local newspaper came from Laurie Riggs, wife of the pastor of Union Congregational Church, located in neighboring North Aurora and not far from the Hindu site. She offered a biblical warning: "I, for one, am frightened by the erection of temples to other gods. When Israel as a nation did that [in the Bible], God had to chasten and bring judgment upon their land and people." Moreover, Mrs. Riggs voiced concern about the direction of the American nation: "Are we going to be proud of something that will again take us away from the religion on which this country was founded?"

A few years later, Riggs's husband, Rev. John Riggs, was interviewed for an article written by Terry Muck, editor of the evangelical periodical *Christianity Today*. The article, titled "The Mosque Next Door: How Do We Speak the Truth in Love to Muslims, Hindus, and Buddhists?" prompted a rebuttal in the periodical *Hinduism Today*, titled "A Friendly Open Letter: Inaccurate Reporting on Hinduism in America Prompts Response to *Christianity Today* Article." Said Rev. Riggs to *Christianity Today*:

> Biblically oriented Christians in this community were naturally afraid of the propagation of a polytheistic faith in their community....I thank God for the religious freedom we have in this country. I realize that if we were to deny that to this group, we would be putting our own freedoms in danger. But I wanted to make sure we demonstrated a strong Christian witness in this community and point up the incompatibility of Hindu and Christian beliefs.

Quoted in the rebuttal piece in *Hinduism Today* as well, Rev. Riggs reiterated his distinction between civic freedoms and theological truth claims: "I do believe in freedom of religion but shall not give any quarter to non-Christians." Sidebars 1.1 and 1.2 contain excerpts from the *Christianity Today* and *Hinduism Today* articles.

Plans for the Sri Venkateswara temple came up for review by the Aurora City Council in May of 1985. A week before the hearing, Aurora resident Donna Kalita asked in a letter to the editor of the local newspaper, "Does Aurora want to be known as the 'home of the largest Hindu temple in America' or as a 'God-fearing little city in America?'" She adamantly opposed the presence of "a temple for gods other than the living God of Abraham, creator of all things." The city council hearing featured a stirring debate,

Excerpt from Terry Muck, "The Mosque Next Door: How Do We Speak the Truth in Love to Muslims, Hindus, and Buddhists?"

Aurora, Illinois (pop. 90,000), sits in the middle of small farms, 30 miles west of metropolitan Chicago.... All along Randall Road, the community's northern approach, fields of corn and soybeans guard its rural virginity.

This pastoral calm is rudely violated as one approaches the city's northern limits. There, rising out of the cornfields like a mountain jutting upward from a grassy plain, is a massive Hindu temple with spires that dwarf a Congregational church's white steeple two pastures away.

Source: *Christianity Today* (February 19, 1988): 15.

SIDEBAR 1.2
Excerpt from "A Friendly Open Letter: Inaccurate Reporting on Hinduism in America Prompts Response to *Christianity Today* Article"

You write, "This pastoral calm [of Aurora] is rudely violated [by] a massive Hindu temple with spires that dwarf a Congregational church's white steeple two pastures away." The choice of words conveys not just an "out-of-place" temple but an "intrusive, wrong, threatening" temple. After our talk, we trust it is accurate to say the temple is no more a "violation" of Aurora's bucolic beauty than the nearby church.

Source: *Hinduism Today* (June 4, 1988), http://www.hinduism-today.com/1988/06/1988-06-04.html.

Note: The editors of *Hinduism Today* and *Christianity Today* had a phone conversation before this rebuttal appeared in print.

representing what Mayor David Pierce later characterized as the best and the worst in Aurora's citizenry. Christians took a variety of positions on the proposed Hindu temple and what it symbolized, which continued to play out in the local newspaper long after the council approved the temple's plans.

At least three positions can be identified among Christian participants in this public debate. The first two have already been intimated. The position articulated by Laurie Riggs and Donna Kalita saw the presence of a Hindu temple in Aurora as contravening the will of God and biblical injunctions, and thus it should not be allowed by the citizens and public officials of the city. William W. Penn labeled city council members non-Christians for "knowingly and willingly going against the Holy Bible" in making "a decision that will, if the temple is built, place Aurora in judgment according to God's word." Michael J. Mallette asked, "Is the God of the Bible the one, true God? If so, then we are facing a provoked, jealous, almighty God who has sworn to take vengeance on all disobedience. I, for one, fear that our city is standing on the threshold of a new and dreadful future." In this view, Aurora would be breaking the Bible's commandment against idol worship by allowing the Hindu temple to be built.

A second position in the debate, expressed by Rev. John Riggs (given earlier), shared the theological evaluation of the first position: Hinduism is a false religion that worships false gods. Nevertheless, this second stance recognized the constitutional rights of Hindus to practice their faith and build their temple in Aurora, along with the Christian duty to oppose Hindu truth claims. "Christianity in its true form is a much different religion," wrote Bobbi Rutherford. "It must not be lumped together with the others. However, the Hindu people have every right to build their temple and worship freely and peaceably—without harassment. This is guaranteed them in the Constitution of our great country." Moreover, Ms. Rutherford pointed out a theological justification to her fellow Christians, in addition to the legal one: "Christians who oppose this view should be reminded that God Himself gave man freedom of choice. No one has the right to deny another that choice."

For Ms. Rutherford and others, the new Hindu temple in Aurora offered a missionary opportunity. Jane Jafferi considered "this temple of idolatry...an abomination to God and to us," yet she called upon Christian Aurorans to "stand on God's word to use this situation to bring Him glory and to work in us." Although she prophesied that "Spiritual darkness shall fall on our city and all manner of evil will increase...both in the spiritual realm and in the physical," she did not fear the future: "God is drawing us together as his ambassadors to these who are in darkness....We need not fear, brothers and sisters in Jesus. We know how the book ends. We're on the winning side."

Pastor Charles Rinks of Souls Harbor Open Bible Church, located a few hundred yards from the Hindu temple property, said, "If I had my 'druthers,' I'd rather them [Hindus] not be here. We ought to say they're here and to show them the superiority of Christianity." Although Pastor Dorothy Brown of Mustard Seed Tabernacle Bible Church, also near the temple, viewed Hinduism as a cult, she did not oppose the presence of Hindus in Aurora. "I tell my congregation to pray for the Hindus, that their understanding be enlightened so they can see the only true God, our father Jehovah," she explained. The Reverend Stephen Miller, pastor of Christian Fellowship Bible Church, taught his congregation to support religious freedom for all but also to stand up for the truth of only one religion, Christianity. "The more people I can affect with the truth," Rev. Miller said, "the less people the Hindus will reach."

The pastor of Aurora First Assembly of God, Rev. Larry Hodge, characterized himself both as "an American who cherishes freedom and as a Christian who serves the Christ." With respect to the first point, "As long as the owners of [the Hindu temple] meet the legal requirements for construction, they should be allowed to build whatever they choose." With respect to the second point, wrote Rev. Hodge, "I must stand in opposition to the teaching and practices the owners of this property will bring to this community. Their teaching and practices produce no real spiritual hope or lasting social redemption." Come what may, Rev. Hodge pledged "to proclaim Jesus Christ as the only hope for this world and its inhabitants."

From the nearby town of Plano, Rev. Paul Dobbins admitted that it would be disconcerting for many Christians to bump into "what the Old Testament calls a 'foreign god,' right in your city's back yard." Even so, he suggested that America's monotheistic Judeo-Christian heritage would resist "pagan" trends like Hindu polytheism. "It will simply be more important than ever," wrote Rev. Dobbins, "for all of us to think more clearly so that in the give and take of ideas among a free people, which we should be glad to be, the best elements of our way of life may have the best opportunity to prevail."

Also attending the Aurora City Council hearing was Rev. Man Singh Das, a former Hindu who was converted by Presbyterian missionaries in India and then became a Methodist minister. The Reverend Das came away "shocked to hear irrational viewpoints expressed by a small group of Aurorans in the name of Christianity," including fears about rat infestation and drug abuse in Hindu temples. He led a three-part seminar organized by the Church and Society Committee of Westminster Presbyterian Church (USA) in Aurora in order to present an accurate understanding of Hinduism. "We should accept the temple, not their teachings," Rev. Das advised his fellow Christians. Ethnocentric bigotry has no place in a Christian approach: "I want to win the soul [of the Hindu]. But, before winning the soul, I want to win his heart."

As we have seen, Christians who agreed about the falsity of Hinduism took two different positions on the presence of a Hindu temple in Aurora. Some sought to prevent the erection of the temple, citing biblical injunctions against idolatry and the potential for divine retribution on the city and its inhabitants, while others recognized both the temple's legal right to exist and its members as a missionary field. A third Christian position considered the proposed Hindu temple a positive contribution to a diverse community. "We welcome the temple as adding to the cultural and religious diversity that we all treasure so highly as Americans and as citizens of Aurora," wrote four local Lutheran pastors in a joint letter to the editor. They also expressed chagrin over the controversy: "We suffer Christian embarrassment and deplore the bigotry that has been expressed, often by persons of the Christian faith. We see this kind of sanctimonious self-serving as alien to the faith of the church of Christ."

Although these Lutheran pastors shared Rev. Das's concern about the lack of Christian charity exhibited by some Christians, they did not express the missionary goals of Rev. Das and others described earlier. This third Christian position welcomed the Hindu temple without feeling a need to evangelize its members. The Reverend Clara Thompson, pastor of First Baptist Church, deplored what she described as "prejudice raising its ugly head here in Aurora" and equated local Christian opposition to Hindus with anti-Semitism in Nazi Germany. "Aurora is not a Christian city," Rev. Thompson argued. "It is a city that has Christians in it, as well as Jewish people, Hindus, other religions or non-believers in any religion. If Hindus should not be here because they are not Christians, how about these others, and how about people who say they are Christians but don't act like it?"

Some Christians advocated reaching out to the local Hindu community in formal dialogue about the beliefs and practices of Hinduism. For instance, a contingent of fifty members of New England Congregational Church, a United Church of Christ congregation, toured the temple when it opened, slipping off their shoes before entering the worship area, which featured images of Sri Venkateswara and several other male and female deities. The Reverend Marshall Esty, a United Methodist minister, suggested that Christians could learn valuable lessons from Hinduism: "The reverence for life that is fundamental to the Hindu way of life at its best may prompt us to rethink our life-denying ways." He also advised Christians concerned about a Hindu temple's violating the biblical commandment against idol worship that Jesus had identified two other commandments as the greatest of all, namely, "you shall love the Lord your God with all your heart and mind and soul and strength. This is the first and great commandment. And the second is like it: You shall love your neighbor as yourself." William Balek asked, "Have those who so bitterly oppose this [temple] in the name of God forgotten that the Bible teaches us that we are all God's children?" He continued: "Those who deny the establishment of another home of worship in the name of Jesus seem to have forgotten that His teachings were those of love and tolerance."

In the Aurora Hindu temple controversy, the notion of tolerance carried both civic and theological connotations. Most of the

SIDEBAR 1.3
Aurora, Illinois, 1985 and 2003

In November of 1985 the *Beacon-News* reported on a public forum organized by the local chapter of the American
Association of University Women. The following is an excerpt
from the article: "An Indian woman and the mayor of Aurora
told an audience Wednesday what they could expect when the
proposed Hindu temple becomes reality. Taken together, their
message was that the temple, being built for a religion very
unlike Christianity, would some day be as commonplace as the
nearly 100 other churches in the city."

The Aurora Hindu temple was consecrated in June of 1986
with the installation of the images of several Hindu deities. In
March of 2003 a major addition to the temple was opened, and
in June of that same year the entire facility was reconsecrated
with five days of religious ceremonies, which drew an estimated
five thousand Hindus from across the country on the final day.
The local newspaper's coverage of the 2003 activities stimulated
no public response.

Christian participants in the debate acknowledged the importance of civic toleration of religious diversity as guaranteed by
law and established in mainstream American culture. Theological
toleration proved a complicated matter, however. A small minority of local Christians—vocal and controversial but still a small
minority—considered Hinduism's beliefs and practices so intoler-
ably false as to abrogate any expectation of civic acceptance. For
them, the Hindu temple simply must not be built under any circumstances. Other Christians combined theological intolerance
with civic open-mindedness—Hinduism is a false religion, but the
Hindu temple had a right to be built. For these Christians, truth,
not tolerance, was the highest theological consideration, and thus
acceptance of religious untruth constitutes no virtue. Yet other

Christians welcomed Hindus both theologically and civically—differences in religious truth claims should be respected and the Hindu temple had a right to be built. These Christians went beyond mere tolerance to express positive appreciation of Hinduism.

Back in May of 1985, on the day of the Aurora City Council hearing, the local newspaper published its stance on the controversy surrounding the proposed Hindu temple. The editorial stressed the legal and economic issues of the case and argued that the temple made "good sense" on both counts. The editorial urged those who attended the hearing to understand that this was "not a religious issue." But, of course, it was a religious (or theological) issue to many, in addition to being about other issues.

In chapter 11 of this book, we revisit the case of the Christians of Aurora, Illinois, and bring their story down to the present time. For a preview, see sidebar 1.3.

For More Information

Terry Muck, "The Mosque Next Door: How Do We Speak the Truth in Love to Muslims, Hindus, and Buddhists?" *Christianity Today* (February 19, 1988): 15–20. Written by then editor of *Christianity Today*, who holds a PhD in comparative religion and participates in an ongoing Buddhist-Christian dialogue among scholars, this article presents an evangelical Christian perspective on the growing religious multiplicity in the United States. Muck elaborates his views in a later book, *Those Other Religions in Your Neighborhood: Loving Your Neighbor When You Don't Know How* (Grand Rapids, Mich.: Zondervan, 1992).

"A Friendly Open Letter: Inaccurate Reporting on Hinduism in America Prompts Response to *Christianity Today* Article," *Hinduism Today* (June 4, 1988), http://www.hinduismtoday.com/1988/06/1988-06-04.html, is a rebuttal to Terry Muck's *Christianity Today* piece by a Hindu periodical.

Christian denominations take a range of positions on Hinduism and other non-Christian religions. The Southern Baptist Convention

(SBC), the nation's largest Protestant denomination, emphasizes evangelism and critique of non-Christian religious truth claims. Access the SBC's Web site at http://www.sbc.net and type the word "Hindu" into the SBCSearch function to retrieve statements about that religion. The United Methodist Church (UMC) emphasizes interfaith dialogue and networking rather than a critique of truth claims. Access the UMC's "Creating Interfaith Community" Web page at http://gbgm-umc.org/missionstudies/interfaith/index.html for general information; Hinduism is included under the "Faith Traditions" section. In a statement titled "Christ and the Other Religions," the Vatican's Pontifical Council for Interreligious Dialogue includes a brief outline of Hindus' responses to Christian presentations of Christ (http://www.vatican.va/jubilee_2000/magazine/documents/ju_mag_01031997_p-29_en.html).

The full name of the Aurora Hindu temple is Sri Venkateswara Swami Temple of Greater Chicago. Its Web site, http://www.balaji.org, offers a virtual tour of the temple and its deities and features photos of the temple's priests, identified by the markings on their foreheads as devoted to the deities Vishnu (a V-shaped mark) or Shiva (horizontal lines). Information about other Hindu temples in the United States can be found on the Web site of the Council of Hindu Temples of North America, http://councilofhindutemples.org. The council's list of temples includes the Dallas–Fort Worth Hindu Temple Society, whose Web site has an interactive "online puja [worship]" feature that allows worshipers to perform virtual rituals to various deities. For a scholarly treatment of American Hinduism see Prema A. Kurien, *A Place at the Multicultural Table: The Development of an American Hinduism* (New Brunswick, N.J.: Rutgers University Press, 2007).

For Discussion

1. Discuss the theological and civic issues involved in the public debate over the presence of a Hindu temple in Aurora, Illinois. Which of the three positions do you think represents the majority of Christians in your community? The three positions are (a) prevent the erection of

the Hindu temple; (b) recognize both the temple's legal right to exist and its members as a missionary field; and (c) welcome the temple without evangelizing its members.

2. Which of the quotations from the Aurora Christians mentioned in this chapter resonates most positively with you? Which resonates most negatively? What would you have written in a letter to the editor of the Aurora newspaper at the height of the controversy in 1985?

3. What do you make of the public silence over the Aurora Hindu temple in 2003? Why was there no heated debate among Christians comparable to that in 1985? Do you think the same positions exist today in Aurora's churches?

4. One letter to the editor in 1985 reminded Aurora Christians of the other temple in town, Temple B'nai Israel, a Conservative synagogue established in 1904. Do the Christian positions described in this chapter apply equally to Hindu temples and Jewish synagogues? Or does Christianity's special historical and theological relationship with Judaism make a difference?

5. Selected Bible passages that underlie the three Christian responses to the proposed Hindu temple in Aurora, Illinois, are the following: (1) Ban the idolatrous presence: Exodus 20:3–6; Deuteronomy 29:16–21; 2 Kings 17:7–23; Isaiah 44:6–20; Hosea 5:4–7; (2) evangelize the newcomers: Matthew 28:18–20; John 3:16–18; John 14:6; Acts 2:38–39; Acts 8:26–40; (3) learn about Hinduism: Amos 9:7; Malachi 1:11; Luke 7:9; John 1:9; John 10:16.

TWO

Evangelizing Fellow Immigrants: South Asian Christians

THE ASIAN AMERICAN POPULATION OF metropolitan Chicago has increased dramatically since the revision of federal immigration laws in the 1960s. The 2000 census counted nearly four hundred thousand Asians in the six-county region, a 52 percent increase over the previous census. South Asians, mostly from India and Pakistan, make up a significant proportion of Chicago's overall Asian population and represent a remarkable religious diversity that includes Hindus, Muslims, Christians, Sikhs, Jains, and others. South Asian Christian churches represent a variety of denominational and theological identities, such as Baptists, Catholics, Evangelicals, Methodists, Lutherans, Mar Thoma, Orthodox, and Pentecostals.

This chapter highlights some initiatives of South Asian Christians to evangelize fellow South Asian immigrants in metropolitan Chicago, often in cooperation with nonimmigrant evangelical groups and volunteers. We examine three cases: (1) Indian evangelists, (2) Telugu Lutheran congregations, and (3) a South Asian Christian community center.

Indian Evangelists

One day a few years ago, evangelist John Bushi went into a small gift shop run out of Suburban Mennonite

Church[1] to see whether it carried any items from his native India. The church eventually appointed Rev. Bushi as its minister of evangelism, specializing in low-profile outreach to immigrant Indians throughout metropolitan Chicago.

Although Suburban Mennonite Church is predominantly white, it is beginning to reflect the growing ethnic and racial diversity of its locale. The church has made overtures to nearby Hindu and Muslim congregations, though no institutional relationships have yet materialized. The pastor saw Rev. Bushi's evangelistic approach as compatible with the congregation's views on outreach:

> What he is trying to do is build relationships so that there are comfortable, natural ways to share Christian faith with the others who are in his fellowship.... Our whole church is based on the concept that we don't exist for ourselves; we exist to reach out to others who need Christ, who need a church home where they feel loved and accepted, or who are seeking, seekers looking for something.

An ordained minister of the Indian Baptist Mission, a union of missionary Baptist denominations in India, Rev. Bushi found the Mennonite tradition amenable to his evangelical concern for his fellow Indian immigrants: "Mennonites believe in helping people, at the same time being with God, which I like very much. When you don't care for the human being who is suffering next door and just talk about religion, that makes no sense. Mennonites are very helping and kind and supporting." Today Rev. Bushi is also a licensed Mennonite minister.

His approach is simple and direct but not overtly religious initially. He invites Indian families to attend informal social get-togethers, where they share food, songs, games, and other activities that help to form a close relationship within the group. He seeks out potential attendees at libraries, gas stations, airports, and other public places and also posts fliers in Indian businesses

---

1. Suburban Mennonite Church is pseudonymous, at the request of Rev. John Bushi.

and scans newspaper ads for Indian names. He even attends local Hindu temples, where he is careful not to give offense in any way.

After a couple of get-togethers, Rev. Bushi begins to probe deeper topics, especially spirituality and family life. One group that meets in Chicago's western suburbs comprises newlyweds experiencing marital problems. "We want to bring them together and show how they can make their lives better with the help of God," Rev. Bushi told us. Many Indian immigrants have lost their jobs since the events of September 11, 2001. "Every family has gone through some problems. So my presence is meant to encourage them constantly and pray with them and see how God can help them with their lives."

In addition, Rev. Bushi trains others to carry on this work by running workshops for what he calls his "core group." They study the Bible together, discuss practical aspects of evangelism, and focus "on how God has helped us in our lives." He freely shares what God did for him when he found himself languishing in an Indian prison in 1980. His mother wrote him a letter, "You have tried all your possible ways, why don't you try God? Why don't you pray?" "So that night I prayed," he told us, "and I had a peace. And a miracle happened, that I was released without any charges." He went on to earn an engineering degree, work in a scientific research institute, and complete a master's degree in theology from United Theological College in Bangalore, India. He draws from his scientific background in conversations with young Indian immigrants who work in engineering, computer technology, and similar fields, calling his approach "creative evangelism for the twenty-first century."

In recent years Rev. Bushi has sensed a significant attitude shift within the immigrant Hindu community. He feels that the early immigrants tried to assimilate to America's dominant Christian culture by downplaying their Hindu identity and practices in order to fit in. However, he believes that both a societal rise in secularism and a tolerance for religious diversity have emboldened Hindus:

> [Society] says you can believe in any god, so we have religious freedom. They say that there is no need of prayer in the schools, at Christmastime don't use Christ's name in any public places, and even the Supreme Court takes out the

Ten Commandments. So these guys [Hindus] get some kind of encouragement, "OK, we can have our own idols; we can have our practice." So they become stronger and stronger. And Hindus never stop at one place. If they are allowed to go in an evangelistic way, they will try to change and convert people because they also believe in the same kind of conversion that we talk about.

In addition, Rev. Bushi identified several strategies that Hindu temples use to attract new members, such as free medical care, classical Indian dance classes, and yoga instruction. He sees this Hindu assertiveness as a harbinger of ill for the United States. "I take it seriously that this country is blessed because of prayers and [Christian] values. But slowly these values are going away because people are not paying attention. So once these idol worshipers come and bring evil things into the society, then probably we will face a lot of problems."

When Rev. Bushi was on staff at Suburban Mennonite Church, his Indian fellowship participated in a number of joint activities with the larger congregation. One lay leader of the larger group of worshipers wanted to see more such interaction. He once crashed a gathering of Indian youth and was impressed by the testimonies he heard. "I was just drawn in—so intriguing—and I was so amazed at some of the stories that I was hearing," he explained to us. "I was an outsider crashing their party, but I felt like I was welcome there. And I encouraged them to tell the same stories that they told each other to the rest of the congregation, so that we could be more intimately involved as a big family. As much as I was blessed by hearing these stories, I figured the bigger congregation could be, too."

Moreover, Rev. Bushi works closely with other Indian evangelists in the Chicago area. Following Rev. Bushi's social evangelism approach, Rev. Jai Prakash Masih started an Indian fellowship at another Mennonite church in the suburbs. "Religious diversity is the reality of the world," he told us. "One cannot deny it. The most appropriate response is Jesus' mandate: Go out and preach." Nonetheless, Indian evangelists must adopt the right attitude in interacting with fellow immigrants:

Personally, I draw on the concept of respect. [Jesus and the apostles] called us to share our faith. To share is not to belittle or condemn; it is to love, not judge....You need to begin with where people are; you cannot bring them to your turf but [must begin] on their own turf. Missions in the traditional way have been misused and have colonial implications. Missions should be based on the mandate of love, to reach out, not bringing people [to] where you are.

Another local Indian evangelist, who goes by the name of Pastor G. John, heads up the Chicago Bible Fellowship, which meets in various rented facilities. He feels called to correct the false "human assumptions" of other religions, like the concepts of reincarnation in Hinduism and nirvana in Buddhism. By contrast, "[Christian] doctrines are not made on human assumptions," he explains:

We have proof, and that proof is the Lord Jesus. See, like a seed he was buried, and he disappeared like water, and when he rose again, he did not come as a monkey or some other disciples [via reincarnation]. Jesus died; Jesus was buried; Jesus rose again. So that is what the Bible says. It is a blessed hope, a living hope, a good hope. So, if I die, I will rise again. This kind of message is preached to non-Christians.

Although such preaching might be perceived as confrontational, Pastor G. John knows that it must be carried out with respect. He likes Rev. Bushi's approach because of its patience and hospitality—when the time is right, you can give your testimony to people without hurting them, while still telling them the truth of the Gospel. He also knows that in the end, only God can convict human hearts:

Yeah, we preach Christ, but we know by experience that we cannot change anybody. If I have power to change people, maybe within a week I change the whole city of Chicago. We depend on God, God does, we trust 100 percent. See, Lord Jesus said in John 15:5, "You can do nothing without me." So we know by experience that we cannot change any people, but we preach. That is our responsibility. The rest, he has to change people.

Telugu Lutheran Congregations

The Reverend John Bushi contrasts his semi-itinerant ministry to those of the established Indian pastors of the Chicago area. One such is Rev. Shadrach Katari, who pastors two Telugu (south Indian) Missouri Synod Lutheran congregations, Bethesda Asian Indian Mission Society on Chicago's north side and Wesley Church Chicago in a near-west suburb. Despite differences of venue, pastors like Rev. Katari share much in common with the Indian evangelists we have considered thus far.

The Reverend Katari often accepts invitations to speak about Christianity to religious and secular groups within the Indian immigrant community. He will not participate in non-Christian worship services due to the Missouri Synod's prohibition against religious syncretism (see chapter 5). He believes that, although other religions contain ethical teachings similar to those of Christianity, "we have only Christ to save us from sin." He finds Hindus more receptive to the Gospel than Muslims since Islam does not accept the divinity of Christ. Hindus are more likely to believe in Christ as a divine savior, a familiar notion in their religion.

The Reverend Katari has written a series of evangelistic tracts that he and members of his congregations distribute to Hindus, especially along Devon Avenue in the heart of the South Asian community on Chicago's north side. One calls Jesus "the Great Guru" and assures Hindus that his death frees them from the effects of karma. Another tract discusses the Hindu concept of *moksha*, ultimate liberation from the human condition. According to Rev. Katari, "their *moksha* is to go into God and become God, oneness in God. But our *moksha* is like the Kingdom of God, and it is different. We have our individuality from God, and we can recognize ourselves. I can explain to them what is *moksha* and how we enjoy *moksha*, how we got peace in *moksha*, like that. So, I translated the Kingdom of God into *moksha*."

In evangelizing the Indians he meets on Devon Avenue, Rev. Katari adopts a personal approach, a strategy he learned while in seminary in India. "When I go, it's a busy street; they are buying groceries. I find people who are sitting on benches and at tables…and I make friendship with them.…I ask them what they are doing, like that. Then I talk about Jesus Christ, and they talk about their religion. I explain how Jesus came to this world and how he saved our souls from sin and condemnation." Such street evangelism can be difficult in India. "God gave us a chance to talk to them in America," says Rev. Katari. "In India, sometimes we don't have a chance to talk like that. Now we do. So, in our case, in this free country, we are able to talk."

He also explains that caste distinctions must be considered when evangelizing fellow Indian immigrants. Many Indian Christians come from the lower castes as a result of the history of Christian missions in India. When Rev. Katari witnesses to upper-caste Hindus, he takes what he calls a more "theoretical" approach by discussing Hindu scriptures and doctrines. With lower-caste Hindus, he discusses "practical" aspects of Hinduism, like its rituals.

Vijay Eanuganti is a member of Rev. Katari's congregation on Chicago's north side. He interacts with Indian Hindus and Muslims on a daily basis, sometimes in the taxi he drives for a living and often in Indian restaurants. Like his pastor, Vijay uses the word "friendship" to describe his approach to fellow Indian immigrants. "If I go to lunch, I sit like one hour," he told us. "Every day, new people are coming, and with them I am doing friendship. I am trying to invite them to church."

In one case, Vijay developed a friendship with a Hindu man who had failed the city cab-driver examination twice. Although the man had driven a taxi in India, he found the exam here very difficult and began to despair of ever passing. Someone told the man to call Vijay for help. Vijay recalls the man saying over the phone, "Oh, I am very scared about my examination." Vijay replied, "Okay, come to my church on Sunday." And the man did. "The pastor prayed for him, and I prayed for him," Vijay told us. "The third time, by the grace of God, he has passed [the exam]. So he was very faithful to God [after that]. Every Sunday he comes [to church]."

Vijay shares such testimonies with the people he encounters. "Now I call all people to the church to just, what do you call, to praise the Lord. I give a statement here. When I came [to the United States], I had nothing. When I came here the Lord blessed me....I tell them, if you also believe in this Lord Jesus Christ, he is going to bless your people also."

Devon Avenue Christian Community Center

Located in the heart of the South Asian community on Chicago's north side, among the myriad Indian restaurants, sari shops, Indo-Pakistani grocery stores, and other ethnic businesses stands the Devon Avenue Christian Community Center (DACCC)[2], an evangelistic outreach ministry that provides Christian literature, children's activities, tutoring, small-group fellowship opportunities (especially for women), English-as-a-second-language instruction, immigrant social services, and Christian worship services for the neighborhood. The DACCC is supported by evangelical churches and colleges throughout the Chicago area that contribute financial assistance and volunteer staff. Even so, this is primarily an outreach by South Asian Christians to their fellow immigrants (see sidebars 2.1 and 2.2).

Assistant director Paul Kelvin, who is not a South Asian, explained DACCC's basic approach, including its implications for nonimmigrant volunteers: "There is a method of evangelism called 'friendship evangelism.' Through our natural contacts as friends, we share our faith just as one friend might share with another. That is how we cross over, as well as be a friend to the community, by giving, by sharing Christ's love through activities for kids and ESL and all those things through the center, those activities of outreach."

Paul likes a phrase he read somewhere, "building bridges of friendship that bear the weight of truth":

2. The names of Devon Avenue Christian Community Center and individuals associated with it are pseudonymous, at the center's request.

SIDEBAR 2.1

Excerpt from the Devon Avenue Christian Community Center Newsletter: "Reaching Hindu Immigrants"

In 1998 the Swaminarayan Temple in Bartlett, Illinois, began a new venture for the South Asian community in Chicagoland.... It is said that, when the construction is finished, it will be the largest Hindu temple outside of India....

We are concerned about reaching the lost for Christ, and what a wonderful blessing from God to bring our work home to us. In the next few years, six more Hindu temples are expected to be built in Chicagoland.

How are we going to reach them in our own communities?

SIDEBAR 2.2

Excerpt from the Devon Avenue Christian Community Center Newsletter: "Telecasting the Cricket World Cup"

Cricket Update: In our spring newsletter we shared about the recent breakthrough in reaching out to Muslim and Hindu men in the Devon Ave. area through telecasting the Cricket World Cup at [the center]. The final tallies are in: The men continued to flood in to [the center], especially when India and/or Pakistan played.... Nearly 500 different men attended the telecasts, with the highest count for one night at 100. About 250 "JESUS" videos were given out in various languages. Some refused the videos, but many accepted them with thanks. The location barrier was broken, and the men are no longer afraid to come to [the center].

I think that sums up what we do.... [Such] friendship is
understanding culture, you know, take off your shoes, all of
those things, learning the basics of what [another] culture
respects, things that might offend. The idea is not to build
walls between that person and yourself by not understanding
anything about them. If there are fewer walls, then they are
more willing to listen to what you have to say about your
faith.

Paul monitors his nonimmigrant volunteers closely to make
sure they do not step on any "cultural toes": "Our underlying message is that we respect each other, and we are not forcing anything
on anybody. We are just sharing with people what we believe. If the
person responds, that is up to them."

One interesting gesture of respect came in response to criticism from Muslims in the neighborhood. Each year at the Indian
Independence Day parade along Devon Avenue, Christian groups
distribute hundreds of evangelistic tracts, most of which are dis-
carded by parade-goers. Some Muslims expressed dismay that
Christians would allow passages from the Bible to be trampled in
the street. Now the DACCC mobilizes volunteers to pick up the
tracts so as not to offend the Muslims' sensitivities about scripture.
(Muslims respect the Bible since it is associated with the prophets
Moses and Jesus, thus making Jews and Christians fellow Peoples
of the Book.)

For the same reason, the Bible is displayed in a prominent
place in the DACCC's bookshop, as Radha Sanghat, an Indian
woman, explained to us: "When you come into the bookstore,
you will see that the Bible is on the highest shelf. The reason
is that Hindu people revere their religious books. So we don't
have a casual attitude towards the Word of God. You will never
see us sitting on our Bible; you will never see a Bible put on the
floor."

"We try to do things in an ethnic way," Radha continued. "We
dress like the community does; we dress very modestly. We are all
things to all people for the sake of the Gospel, like [the apostle]
Paul said, without compromising the Gospel. So we bring about
outer changes, which makes them feel welcome and accepted,

and once they are in, the love of Christ wins them over." This culture-sensitive approach includes respecting many traditional South Asian views on gender. Men and women sit separately at the center's worship services "because that is how God is worshiped in Hinduism and in Islam. Women and men are separated. They are very reverent in worship, so we cover our heads, too. We make it as easy as possible for them, so that the outer [behavior] does not disgust them. Offenses are kept to a minimum," Radha explained.

Radha directs the women's programs at the DACCC. The center has created a haven for many South Asian women, some of whom experience spousal abuse and other family problems:

> When they came to us and they found us loving them and treating them with kindness, respect, and dignity, they started opening up to us and sharing. We became a safe place for us [South Asian women]. As they started sharing their problems, that is when we started expanding and helping them wherever we could. And through word of mouth we have grown. . . . When women come in here they are isolated; they don't have community. We helped by doing ladies' luncheons and inviting the other women from the community. So within community, they built community, got to know each other and developed friendships.

Radha spoke of one woman who was about to undergo an abortion. Through the prayers and friendship of women at the DACCC, the woman decided to have the baby, "this precious little one," as Radha says. "The woman is a friend, and she brings her baby, and all of us love her. She has found community in us."

"What we do is friendship evangelism," Radha echoes Paul Kelvin, the DACCC's assistant director. "Here is our policy: We live the Gospel, and once others live it, then they will believe it. That is why this is a friendship center. . . . We want to be the aroma, the love, and the hands and feet of Jesus in the community. We live the Gospel first, and then we give it vocally."

Sanjay Pandya, an Indian man, volunteers his time at the DACCC. He agrees with this quiet, friendly approach to his non-

Christian fellow immigrants. When we asked him how American Christians should respond to the growing number of non-Christian immigrants generally, he replied, "The response is not to condemn; the response is to love and accept them. We need to be different, to show them that there is a difference in us....We shouldn't be condemning and saying that you are wrong. No, we should love them."

Sanjay told us of a person that he regularly accompanies on walks around the neighborhood, during which time he shares what Jesus has done for him and prays for the person when asked. "That's all I do now. I don't speak anything more. I leave it to the Lord. He will do what he has to." Fewer words, more Christian love—that's his approach nowadays. "Love, that's it. Love, and meet the needs. Don't speak too much; just meet the needs. A lot of people are hurting."

Sanjay says he came to know the Lord in 1978. "Then I realized what was the truth." He also realized something that other new immigrant Christians share: "Usually it's your own people you feel for first."

For More Information

Padma Rangaswamy, *Namaste America: Indian Immigrants in an American Metropolis* (University Park: Pennsylvania State University Press, 2000), paints a comprehensive portrait of the Indian immigrant experience in Chicago. For an in-depth look at the religious diversity of the South Asian population in the United States, see two books by Raymond Brady Williams, *Religions of Immigrants from India and Pakistan: New Threads in the American Tapestry* (New York: Cambridge University Press, 1988) and *Christian Pluralism in the United States: The Indian Immigrant Experience* (New York: Cambridge University Press, 1996).

The Federation of Indian American Christian Organizations of North America (FIACONA) is a watchdog organization for Christian rights in India. Contact them at FIACONA, 110 Maryland Avenue

NE, Suite 306, Washington, D.C. 20002; phone 202-547-6228; email info@fiacona.org; http://www.fiacona.org.

Information about Rev. Shadrach Katari's ministry to Telugu Lutherans can be found at his Web site, http://www.geocities.com/shadrachkatari.

For Discussion

1. In this chapter we see immigrants and nonimmigrants cooperatively evangelizing South Asians. What advantages and disadvantages might each group have in this work? Do you think non-Christian South Asians would be more open to evangelization by fellow immigrants or by nonimmigrants? How important is it not to step on "cultural toes" when dealing with immigrant religious groups?

2. Discuss the "social evangelism" or "friendship evangelism" approach. Are you comfortable with it? What are its strengths and weaknesses? Do you think it would be difficult for an evangelical Christian to maintain a friendship with a person who does not respond to invitations to become a Christian? What is the proper balance between "doing" and "preaching" the Gospel?

3. Recall this statement by Rev. John Bushi: "Hindus never stop at one place. If they are allowed to go in an evangelistic way, they will try to change and convert people because they also believe in the same kind of conversion that we talk about." Discuss the implications of multiple new religious groups with conversionary agendas encountering each other in the United States. Can they all get along? Does this situation strengthen or weaken American society?

4. Are adherents of some religions inherently more receptive to the Gospel than others due to certain beliefs? Recall Rev. Shadrach Katari's view that Hindus are more receptive than Muslims. Are there other avenues of receptivity besides similarities of beliefs? Discuss obstacles to receptivity as well, such as Islam's rejection of the divinity of Jesus Christ.

5. Bible passages: Pastor G. John says John 15:5 gives him perspective in his evangelistic work by reminding him that it is ultimately Jesus who changes people. The Reverend Shadrach Katari, the Lutheran pastor, contrasts the Kingdom of God to the Hindu concept of *moksha,* or ultimate liberation from the human condition. Look at the Kingdom of God/Heaven parables in Matthew 13 and the parable of the workers in the vineyard in Matthew 20:1–15.

THREE

Resettling for Christ: Evangelical Churches of DuPage County

IN THE PREVIOUS CHAPTER WE saw South Asian Christians evangelizing fellow immigrants, sometimes with the aid of nonimmigrant churches and volunteers. In this chapter we focus on the efforts of nonimmigrant churches to evangelize non-Christian immigrants and refugees from a variety of countries who are resettling in suburban DuPage County, west of Chicago. Here, too, "friendship evangelism" plays an important role, this time across both religious and ethnic boundaries.

A key participant in these efforts is World Relief DuPage, the local arm of the international nongovernmental organization World Relief, which in turn is the humanitarian arm of the National Association of Evangelicals (see sidebar 3.1). Active in twenty countries, World Relief provides a variety of services in areas such as health, poverty, agriculture, and emergency relief. Self-consciously motivated by evangelical principles, World Relief supports congregations in relieving local suffering. While World Relief itself does not directly evangelize the beneficiaries of its services, it also does not discourage its local church partners from doing so.

World Relief DuPage began providing services for refugees and immigrants in DuPage County in 1979 and expanded into adjacent Kane County twenty years later by opening a branch office in Aurora. Refugee resettlement has become World Relief DuPage's main emphasis, a difficult task given the typically traumatic

SIDEBAR 3.1
Excerpts from "The Story of the Church at Work"

World Relief believes that the church must be the "hands of Jesus."

Matthew 5:16 says: "Let your light shine before men, that they may see your good deeds and praise your Father in heaven." And James 1:22 says: "Do not merely listen to the word.... Do what it says."

The Mission of World Relief, as originated within the National Association of Evangelicals, is to work with, for, and from the church to relieve human suffering, poverty, and hunger worldwide in the name of Jesus Christ.

Source: http://www.wr.org/aboutus/vision.asp.

refugee experience. "The primary focus of this program is to assist refugees, who have fled war, torture, and persecution, to resettle in the United States with U.S. government approval," explains an information sheet. "Our model of service is to link newly arriving refugees with community volunteers and churches to assist them in the process of adjusting to their new life."

Approximately 80 percent of World Relief DuPage's budget comes from government contracts to resettle refugees brought to the area by the U.S. State Department. Prior to 2001, the agency resettled an average of four hundred refugees per year in DuPage County (in the aftermath of the events of September 11, 2001, the U.S. government has significantly restricted refugee admissions). At the time of our research, World Relief DuPage was preparing for a large contingent of Muslim Bantus, an especially needy group from Somalia, who, according to World Relief sources, will become the largest African refugee group ever resettled in the United

States. In just one quarter of 2008, World Relief DuPage resettled families from Cuba, Eritrea, Iran, Iraq, Myanmar (Burma), the Togolese Republic, and Vietnam.

As a World Relief DuPage representative explained at a church workshop we attended, the majority of the local refugees are currently Muslims, many of whom come from countries where it is difficult for Christian missionaries to operate. This provides an opportunity to evangelize these groups in the United States. "Afghanistan is here, Somalia is here in DuPage County," the representative emphasized, a situation that offers "cross-cultural ministry opportunities right here at home." He gave a slide presentation titled "Missions on Your Doorstep," which suggests two main reasons for churches to get involved:

1. "Worldview expansion" through both discovering God's concern for the poor and developing relationships with people from different cultures; the latter allows American Christians to learn how their own culture influences their understanding and expression of Christianity.

2. "Enlarging people's hearts" by providing services that can benefit volunteers as much as recipients.

Local churches commit to helping refugees through World Relief DuPage's programs at three levels, with increasing investment of volunteers, time, and resources. Level One involves a one-time commitment in order to explore longer-term involvement. At this level, a church may collect items for a refugee family, provide emergency funds, or simply invite a World Relief representative to address the congregation. Level Two involvement is a long-term responsibility that also entails more financial commitment. Activities at this level may include opening church facilities to English-as-a-second-language (ESL) classes and other service programs or organizing fundraisers for refugee aid. Level Three churches commit to substantial programming and financial support on a continuing basis. This may include organizing a Good Neighbor Team, which works closely with a refugee family on matters of temporary housing, transportation, and other day-to-day aspects of the resettlement process. World Relief describes the Good Neighbor Teams as "the hands and feet of Christ to refugees transitioning to self-sufficiency." The World Relief DuPage representative at the workshop explained that the ultimate goal at all three levels is for refugees "to experience a transformation in their lives through a relationship with Jesus Christ." Many volunteers testify to their own transformation as well.

The workshop was sponsored by the Missions Leadership Network, a consortium of local churches that describes itself as "an evangelical interdenominational group interested in seeing the Kingdom move forward." The group's mailing list runs to more than seventy-five entries, several of which work with World Relief DuPage. One of the most committed is Wheaton Bible Church, located in Wheaton, Illinois, the county seat of DuPage County.

Wheaton Bible Church

A few years ago the Missions Festival at Wheaton Bible Church chose as its theme "Connecting in a World of 'Differents.'" Doug Christgau, pastor of cross-cultural ministries at the time of our research, stated that this theme sums up the church's approach to religious diversity. Historically strong in global missions (currently supporting missionary work in forty-two countries), Wheaton Bible Church has expanded its local missions programming significantly in recent years. The Missions Festival brochure put it this way:

> "Differents." [R]efugees, immigrants, international students—
> they are here...and they are different. Saris instead of skirts.
> Sandals instead of shoes. Curry instead of catsup. Hummus
> instead of hash browns. A thousand gods, not one God. Or one
> god, but so very different from the One we know.
>
> Do we smile politely and keep our distance? Or do we
> give our fears to our Protector and connect with these highly
> relational people for the sake of Jesus Christ? At WBC our
> global passion includes bringing the Gospel to those from other
> cultures who have moved right into our neighborhood.

Doug Christgau feels that too few American churches have a vision that extends beyond their own four walls. Those evangelical churches that do have such a vision tend to implement it in other countries through missionary work. Doug hopes to inspire evangelical churches to do "local cross-cultural ministries": "Especially in a globalized world, this is a mandate. We can't just send people over to Africa anymore," he says. Doug calls this "increasing our investment" in sharing the Gospel with the contemporary world.

The guiding rubric of Wheaton Bible Church's extensive work with refugees and immigrants is "friendship ministry" or "friendship evangelism," modeled in part on the work of the Ethnic Focus Ministry of SIM-USA, based in Charlotte, North Carolina (also see chapter 2). The friendship approach is "a very relational ministry," Doug explained:

> We're not assuming that being confrontational about our beliefs or overly prophetic is going to be very well received. We recognize that people can begin to trust us as individuals who care for them regardless of their spiritual convictions and that that concern is going to continue whether they see it our way or not, so to speak. We're going to basically maintain an interest in friendship with people for as long as they give us the opportunity.

Clearly, the ultimate motivation here is evangelism. When we asked Doug how the Gospel is broached in this friendship approach, he talked about earning the right to be heard and about the relationship between the social and spiritual aspects of such work:

> We believe that we have to earn the right to be heard. The way that we earn the right to be heard is by meeting their social needs...recognizing that that has value in itself. A very small percentage of these people end up converting. But we're still committed to helping them....We always have the spiritual objectives in mind, but we know, practically speaking, that that's not going to be realized in the majority of cases. But still these people need our help, and we grow from being of service to them.

Evangelical motivation distinguishes Wheaton Bible Church's approach from that of other social service providers:

> We believe that people who die without a personal relationship with Christ will experience eternal damnation. That's not a very popular position today, but we believe it. So we would say we'd like to address the ultimate needs of the people we're ministering to, not just the immediate needs. The ultimate need is for a spiritual reconciliation with God through Jesus Christ.

Doug is especially moved by Old Testament teachings about showing hospitality to strangers and providing for their practical needs. He notes that the well-known New Testament exhortations to spread the Gospel to all nations often lead churches to focus exclusively on global missions. However, the Old Testament's emphasis on hospitality to the strangers in our midst provides a needed balance of local missionary concern.

Wheaton Bible Church's international friendship ministries include annual holiday meals on Mother's Day, the Fourth of July, and Thanksgiving; skill training classes (currently sewing, with plans to add computer training); and refugee resettlement and ESL programs coordinated by World Relief DuPage. We interviewed three church volunteers deeply involved in these ministries: Thomas Williamson, Helen Anton, and Leanne Margot. All three preferred to be identified by pseudonyms so as not to jeopardize their relationships with those they serve now or may serve in the future. All three also have backgrounds in overseas missions, which provide an important perspective on their work here in the United States.

Thomas Williamson served for twenty-seven years as an overseas missionary. Had we been in certain countries, he told us, he would not have consented to an interview for fear of being misrepresented and perhaps deported. When Tom retired from overseas work several years ago, he and several other retired missionaries searched for a church where they could continue their calling locally. They chose Wheaton Bible Church.

Tom brought a large photo album to our interview and lovingly showed us snapshots of his local work with Afghans, Iranians,

Koreans, and others in the same way that he might share his mementos from some of their home countries. He told stories about refugee families that have stayed in his own home during one crisis or another in their transition to permanent settlement in DuPage County and about the successful careers many have adopted. When we asked Tom what he and other volunteers get out of their work with refugees, he chuckled, "Well, we get a lot of friendships." He also pointed to "what it's added to our family. To see our kids relate to people from other cultures with comfort and joy is worthwhile." The Americans he observed overseas fell into two types, he said, those who chose to live in an American cocoon and those who were open to learning all they could about indigenous cultures. Tom and his family were of the latter type, and they maintain that openness in multicultural America.

Tom draws inspiration from several Bible passages in his work with refugees and immigrants. He points out that, while Christ certainly told his disciples to go out to the world and spread the Gospel, the Holy Spirit brought the whole world to them at Pentecost. Every salvation story in the Book of Acts, Tom says, is about someone who is away from home. Transience makes people more open to the Gospel. Throughout the Bible, God moves people around, taking them from one geography to another and preparing them to be receptive to God's promptings. Tom also draws from Old Testament teachings about the disadvantaged and aliens in the land, as well as the great heavenly scene in the book of Revelation, where all of the nations gather around the throne of God. Tom feels privileged to take part in preparing for that day. He believes that all of the world's languages will be spoken in heaven and that we will then understand them all.

Helen Anton oversees the international friendship ministries of Wheaton Bible Church. She works with a committee of volunteer leaders who in turn deploy dozens of volunteer workers for various programs. When we asked what she thinks her volunteers get out of their work, Helen mentioned "the satisfaction of knowing that they're moving beyond their own comfort level and treating others as God would want them to treat them." Learning the names of the people they serve is usually the first step in overcoming their discomfort in working with unfamiliar groups. "They have a hard time pronouncing the names," Helen explains, "and sometimes that in itself is very threatening." Once they get past such anxieties, the volunteers can begin to see refugees and immigrants as fellow human beings made in the image of God.

According to Helen, the volunteers prize certain biblical teachings, such as the Golden Rule and caring for the needs of the least among us, by which we show our care for Christ himself. For Helen and others who have lived overseas, the Old Testament's passages about how to treat aliens and strangers hold particular power since they know what it means to have that status.

Through it all, volunteers can learn as much about their own faith as anything else. Says Helen, "It's personally enriching just to build friendships with those of another culture. Often I think that helps our own faith to grow in the process because, when we're asked questions about 'Why do you believe this?' or 'What do you believe about this?' it helps us to research more where we're coming from and cement things that maybe we didn't have solid before."

In 1993 Leanne Margot and her husband returned from eleven years of missionary work in Africa. They immediately felt "a huge hole" in their lives. "To be involved with internationals helped [us] fill that void and [deal with] our own 'lostness' as strangers in our own land. There was something familiar about being with people that are of different cultures." Leanne and her husband knew what it felt like to be strangers, so they began to reach out to refugees and immigrants, Leanne as a volunteer home visitor through ESL contacts, and both she and her husband through involvement in Bible study groups. Over the years, several close friendships have developed from these interactions.

Leanne no longer sees her work with refugees and immigrants as a safety net for the lostness she once felt, but it still feels "comfortable and right" to her. She loves being around different foods and worldviews and appreciates the general hospitality of non-Western cultures. Like others we interviewed, Leanne sees the Old Testament's concern for foreigners as a model for her work. As in the case of the biblical Ruth, they were accepted as part of the community. Leanne also pointed out that Jesus was a refugee child in Egypt and, in becoming a human being, can even be considered "displaced" from heaven. "God uses displacement in people's lives to bring about change," she says, from the biblical stories of exiled groups to the lives of refugees and immigrants today. Through such displacement, they may become more willing to seek the truth. Certainly they are hoping to reestablish the bonds of community lost through the traumatic migration process. "We as followers of Christ can offer that to them, to be part of their new community, in the process hopefully pointing the way to a relationship with God."

We asked all three interviewees to estimate how many of the people served by Wheaton Bible Church's friendship evangelism programs eventually find their way to a relationship with God. None could offer an exact percentage, although all agreed that it would be quite low and further stated that "success" does not necessarily depend on numbers. Tom Williamson believes it might take a generation to see the fruits of their present labors. Helen Anton tells volunteers that they are called to be obedient and to let God take care of the rest—even the rich young man of the parable who decided to keep his wealth instead of following Jesus did so in response to Jesus' direct, personal appeal. Leanne Margot explained, "It's a process. I don't know the end of the story. I've only been involved for ten years." Some might get frustrated, but "I don't, really, because that's not my sole motivation. I feel like to be a friend to a stranger is a commandment. I'm commanded to be a light to people. I'm not responsible for their choices." She recalls her friendship with a Chinese man who had been brought up as an atheist in mainland China. Although he and others like him sought more meaning to life than the material world they were taught to believe is the only reality, "they never came to that point that evangelicals often talk about, of a fixed decision [for Christ], and yet I felt like they were in this process.... It wasn't real tangible—where they were actually at."

All three interviewees are committed to the friendship approach. When Tom Williamson is out and about informally, he looks for opportunities to strike up conversations with people who might come from another country. Once, while doing hospital visitations, he began talking with a Hindu nurse and has continued to say hello to her every time he visits the hospital. The key to this relationship, according to Tom, is "just the fact that she's perceived as a person worth talking to." The same is true for the Muslims he knows, who value the personal prayers he offers on their behalf in their presence. "I make it clear that my friendship is not based on anything that they need to do or say [and] that I will be their friend one way or the other." In other words, his friendship has no evangelical strings attached to it. When individuals come back to see him after moving away, "Almost always it's some act of friendship or something informal that has made the impression." For instance, a Liberian physician couple recently told him how much they appreciated the high school graduation reception he gave them at his home.

Helen Anton explained, "Our goal is to build relationships because relationships are where trust is built. If we ever want to earn a hearing for the Gospel, a relationship is vital. You can't just bring in people to preach at them." But when and how to broach the Gospel explicitly can vary, and sometimes the subject does not come up at all. "For the most part, we just try to be there and listen," Helen said. She does not avoid the subject but tries to find natural ways into it. Meals can provide such an entrée, as church volunteers who visit refugee and immigrant homes are often asked to pray before the meal their hosts serve them out of hospitality. "It's a natural thing to do and yet for them a beautiful gift. It's fun to see the big glow on their faces when someone has actually prayed for them." For many, this is the first time they have ever heard their name mentioned in a prayer.

What benefits do refugees and immigrants receive from the efforts of Wheaton Bible Church? Our interviewees pointed to a variety of practical things: learning the language and culture of their new country, gaining access to indigenous advocates and networks for advice and aid, acquiring marketable skills, developing self-esteem, and making friends outside of their own ethnic communities. Leanne Margot explained how important this last point can be. Making American friends can be a barometer of how well a person is adjusting to American society. It can also overcome serious depression. She tells the story of the lonely refugee women from an African culture in which people regularly stop by to visit for no special reason. Who will do this in the United States? Who will come and visit as their new friends?

We observed an ESL class hosted by Wheaton Bible Church, one of several DuPage County churches that work with World Relief DuPage on ESL ministries to refugees and immigrants. On that day, the class met at College Church, just down the street, where other ESL classes were also in session.

World Relief DuPage provided the teacher for the class, Wheaton Bible Church the volunteer assistants. A student teacher from Wheaton College led the class on the day we visited and covered the primary lesson: the difference between simple past tense and present perfect tense. The ESL students, a mix of refugees and immigrants from Latin America, Europe, and Asia, seemed to struggle with the grammatical concepts. (A reminder for English-as-a-first-language readers of this book: The simple past tense expresses an action that occurred once in the past, like "Did you eat snails last night?" whereas the present perfect tense expresses indeterminate past action, like "Have you ever eaten snails?") The students exhibited a range of proficiency in conversational English, from barely comprehensible to relatively skilled, and several spoke to each other in their native tongues during the session. Most appeared cheerfully studious and comfortable with each other. The class met four mornings a week, two hours per session.

The secondary lesson for the day was about so-called reduced forms of phrases. The teacher pointed out that indigenous American speakers tend to contract phrases like "have you" and "did you" into "havya" and "dijya," respectively. If foreign speakers wish to blend into American society and begin speaking with an American ("informal") accent, they need to adopt such reduced forms. The students caught on to this much more quickly than they had the simple past tense versus present perfect tense distinction.

Midway through the session, the class adjourned to the church sanctuary for a half-hour Bible story time with the other classes. This takes place once a week and is optional for the students due to World Relief's restrictions on direct evangelism (the teacher told us that some students opt out, but most attend in order to hear more spoken English). More than one hundred students representing numerous nationalities gathered in the pews. Most wore Western-style clothing (the African women in their native dresses were the exception). A few women from Africa and the Middle East wore the traditional Muslim *hijab* (headscarf).

The religious and moral content of this portion of the day stood in stark contrast to the secular ESL lessons. An amateur troupe of church members acted out the Old Testament story of Jacob and Esau, from the favoritism of their parents (Isaac for Esau, Rebekah for Jacob), to Jacob's treachery in gaining his elder brother's inheritance, to Esau's wrath in response. Some humorous aspects of the play drew hearty laughs from the audience, like stuffing two pillows under Rebekah's blouse to represent Jacob and Esau in the womb. The moral of the story was stated directly: We should not be like Jacob, who wanted to take things that did not belong to him; rather, we should wait for the good gifts God promises to give us.

The narrator of the play concluded with a prayer, for which most of the audience bowed their heads. She thanked God for all of the good gifts of life, especially the gift of God's Son, the Lord Jesus Christ. After the "amen," the audience applauded in appreciation.

For More Information

The Web site of the international relief and social development organization World Relief is http://www.wr.org; World Relief DuPage's Web site is http://dupage.wr.org. The Web site of World Relief's parent organization, the National Association of Evangelicals, is http://www.nae.net.

Wheaton Bible Church's Web site is http://www.wheatonbible.org. Information about the Missions Leadership Network, an interdenominational, evangelical consortium of local churches, can be requested from Wheaton Bible Church, 410 N. Cross Street, Wheaton, IL 60187; phone 630-260-1600.

Ethnic Focus Ministry is a program of SIM-USA, P.O. Box 7900, Charlotte, NC 28241; phone 800-521-6449; Web site http://www.simusa.org/efm. Serving in Mission (SIM) is an interdenominational, evangelical missions organization (http://www.sim.org). For an article by a former SIM-USA director that presents an agenda for domestic ethnic missions, see David L. Ripley, "Reaching the World at Our Doorstep," *Evangelical Missions Quarterly* 30(2) (April 1994), available at http://bgc.gospelcom.net/emis/emqpg. htm. Also see Arthur G. McPhee, *Friendship Evangelism: The Caring Way to Share Your Faith* (Grand Rapids, Mich.: Zondervan, 1978).

Wheaton College (http://www.wheaton.edu), a respected evangelical college in Wheaton, Illinois, houses the Billy Graham Center for evangelism. The center advises churches on evangelizing non-Christians in their locales through its departments of Ethnic Ministries and Ministries to Muslims, as well as its resource and publishing arm, the Evangelism and Missions Information Service (EMIS). Contact the Billy Graham Center, Wheaton College, Wheaton, IL 60187; phone 630-752-5157; e-mail bgcadm@wheaton.edu; http://bgc.gospelcom.net.

Sociological descriptions of several immigrant religious groups can be found in R. Stephen Warner and Judith G. Wittner, eds., *Gatherings in Diaspora: Religious Communities and the New Immigration* (Philadelphia: Temple University Press, 1998), and Helen Rose Ebaugh and Janet Saltzman Chafetz, *Religion and the New Immigrants: Continuities and Adaptations in Immigrant Congregations* (Walnut Creek, Calif.: AltaMira, 2000).

For Discussion

1. Interfaith Refugee and Immigration Ministries (IRIM), an arm of the Illinois Conference of Churches, provides virtually the same social services to refugees and immigrants as does World Relief DuPage and also works with local church sponsors. Compare IRIM's Web site (http://www.irim.org) with the descriptions of World Relief DuPage and Wheaton Bible Church in this chapter. Where does Christian evangelism figure into IRIM's work? What do you think of the various ways the Gospel is broached by the people featured in this chapter?

2. How important is the notion of missions to your congregation? If it is important to you, what is the proper balance of local and global emphases? Do you agree with Doug Christgau of Wheaton Bible Church that churches should step up their local missions?

3. What do you think of the "friendship ministry" or "friendship evangelism" approach after reading this chapter? Do you agree with Thomas Williamson that there are no evangelical strings attached to such friendships? Would recognizing that only God can convict human hearts to accept the Gospel defray the disappointment of friends' resisting evangelistic overtures?

4. Serving in overseas missions gave Thomas Williamson, Helen Anton, and Leanne Margot an important perspective on their work in the United States. Discuss their experiences and their relationships with the refugees and immigrants they serve. Can members of one ethnic group truly understand the experiences of another group?

5. Bible passages: The masthead of World Relief's Web site (http://www.wr.org) once carried this quote from Isaiah 58:10: "If you spend yourselves in behalf of the hungry and satisfy the needs of the oppressed, then your light will rise in the darkness." The World Relief piece titled "The Story of the Church at Work" (see sidebar 3.1) quotes Matthew 5:16 and James 1:22. On the treatment of aliens and strangers in the land, see Exodus 23:9; Leviticus 19:33–34; Deuteronomy 10:17–19, 24:17–18; Psalm 146:9; and Ezekiel 22:7, 29. In Exodus 18:1–4 we read that the name of one of Moses' sons, Gershom, derives from the Hebrew word for "stranger" or "sojourner."

FOUR

Hosting Muslim Neighbors: Calvary Episcopal Church

AS IN DOZENS OF MOSQUES throughout metropolitan Chicago, immigrant Muslims gather at Batavia Islamic Center in far west suburban Kane County every Friday afternoon for a congregational prayer service. They meet in a basement prayer room, its cement floors covered with Oriental rugs and other pieces of carpeting, the area divided into men's and women's sections, with chairs around the perimeter for non-Muslim visitors. The "front" of the room is actually the northeast corner, as indicated by a pulpit and a small accoutrement pointing the direction (following the curvature of the earth from the United States) to Mecca, Islam's holiest city, which all Muslims face in prayer.

As in other Chicago-area mosques every Friday, the faithful at Batavia Islamic Center perform the traditional Islamic prayer rituals, listen to a sermon, and socialize briefly before most of them rush back to their workplaces. They originate from India, Pakistan, and other parts of the Muslim world and follow the majority Sunni tradition of Islam.

But this mosque is unique in one important way: Batavia Islamic Center meets in the basement of a church, Calvary Episcopal Church. It is not unusual for Muslim groups in the United States to purchase former Christian facilities and transform them into mosques. However, at least in Chicago, this is the only case of a functioning church hosting a mosque. And this institutional arrangement has been in place since 1987.

"'Interfaith' is a buzzword now," says Mazher Ahmed, cofounder with her husband, Hamid, of Batavia Islamic Center. "You think, 'Oh my goodness, interfaith—it's a great thing.' But at that time [the 1980s], who knew about interfaith? I don't think people even understood what interfaith was all about. That is why I feel real proud that we have started a tradition and not because of the necessity of 9/11."

Established in downtown Batavia in the 1840s, Calvary Episcopal Church is old by American Midwestern standards. The congregation built an educational wing in the late 1960s in anticipation of an influx of new members from the prestigious Fermi National Accelerator Laboratory on the outskirts of town. However, the expected membership windfall never materialized. Instead of accommodating new Episcopalians, by the late 1980s Calvary Church's extra space would host a growing immigrant Muslim congregation.

The Ahmeds relate the history of the mosque and its relationship with Calvary Church in grateful fashion. When the couple arrived in Batavia from their native India in 1972, they asked Muslim relatives and acquaintances about where the immigrant community gathered for Friday prayers. They were dismayed to discover that most did not perform the Friday prayers on a regular basis. Back then the metropolitan area had only a few mosques, the closest of which was on Chicago's north side, an hour's drive from the far west suburbs.

A Muslim group in Elgin, north of Batavia, soon bought a former church facility and turned it into a mosque, but they did not offer Friday prayers. Hamid Ahmed explains that they were afraid to ask for the time off from work to attend prayers. "But I said no, this country allows you to do your religious stuff," he recalls telling them. He convinced them to allow him to open the mosque for Friday prayers.

Still, the drive to Elgin posed an inconvenience for the Ahmeds and others from Batavia, so the Ahmeds opened their home for the prayer services beginning in 1977. When attendance grew to the point that people were praying in every room on the first floor of the house, the Ahmeds decided it was time for another move. For a year, the congregation used a vacant cabin owned by a private social club in Batavia before outgrowing that space, too.

In the meantime, Hamid inquired among his coworkers in the county government offices about vacant schools the Muslims could rent. Word spread to the county superintendent of schools, Jim Hansen, who called Hamid into his office. Hamid thought Jim wanted him to redraw a school district's boundaries as part of his job in the county mapping department. However, as Hamid and Mazher tell it today, Jim said, "I have in mind a place you can use, but I would like you to see it first. It's a church. Do you think it will be okay if you pray in a church?"

Mazher's reaction was, "Goodness gracious, why not?" Hamid agreed: "A church is God's place." So Jim arranged for the Ahmeds to see his church, Calvary Episcopal Church, and to meet with its rector, Fr. Drury Green.

"They [the Muslim congregation] were looking for space to use," Fr. Green told us. "We had a lot of unused, empty space. It began that way, very easily.... It was a relationship that was rather casual and kind of grew."

Jim Hansen agrees about the serendipity of establishing this relationship between mosque and church. "Hamid always says that I am the one responsible. But it was kind of an indirect, almost by chance thing." One gets the impression that Jim feels he was simply in a position to facilitate the connection. "I explained to Fr. Green who Hamid was. I got them together—that was about it as far as my active participation goes."

Yet Jim Hansen's motivations for helping the Muslim congregation ran deep into his family background and personal philosophy. His mother, who died when Jim was young, loved to help people. His brother worked for agencies of the U.S. government and the United Nations that aided needy groups, for instance, through teacher training in Nigeria. In the 1960s, while Jim served on the Batavia city council, he was instrumental in the passage of an open housing ordinance that benefited the small African American population in town—"a real ordinance with teeth in it," he emphasizes.

When we asked him for his views on religious diversity, Jim said, "I really think it's great that we do this [host the Muslim congregation]....It's a demonstration to the community. These people should be treated in a Christian manner even if they are not Christians." He continued: "I believe in diversity....My own feeling is, diversity, whether it is among Christians or all people, the more we diversify, the better. Even if you don't think they are right. I am not sure that we are right."

Father Drury Green describes Calvary Church as basically open to other religious groups, Christian and non-Christian. Most of the congregation feels that hosting the mosque is simply a good thing to do. Theologically, Fr. Green points to several motivations for the relationship. "Since I was around the building, I always had a lot of informal conversation [with the mosque members]," he told us. "I loved being around the children and young people, who are really a reminder that we are all children of God. Somehow young children are great at doing that just by your contact with them."

"Some of the informal dialogue I had with the [Muslim] community and perhaps others also focused on the idea of being People of the Book. And that Islam and Judaism and the Christian faith all have a common heritage, the Hebrew Scriptures or the Old Testament." Father Green also draws inspiration from the Anglican tradition's *Book of Common Prayer,* particularly the baptismal covenant, at the place where the congregation is asked, "Will you strive for justice and peace among all people and respect the dignity of every human being?" (1979 version). "It seems to me that from a theological standpoint," Fr. Green explained, "respect and dialogue, mutual respect and mutual dialogue are increasingly important....Certainly since 9/11, the Muslim-Christian-Jewish dialogue is even more important. I see this of primary importance not only for the international community but within our own society. We have increasing numbers of people from different religious bodies. In the Chicago area there are Hindus, Buddhists, and Muslims, to name just some."

For the Ahmeds, religious dialogue is a passion. Mazher is a tireless public speaker. When conservative Muslims object to this, Hamid replies that Allah gave his wife a great gift that she should use and that the Qur'an nowhere forbids women to speak in public. ("That usually shuts them up," he told us.) Mazher is also on the executive committee of the Council for a Parliament of the World's Religion and a leader in several Muslim organizations. Passionate about the need for both *intra*faith and *inter*faith dialogue in today's world, she points to the undercurrents of tension within every religious community. "Is interfaith dialogue worthwhile when our home religious communities are so fractured?" she asks. She wants the various Muslim groups, as well as other religions, to "come together as human beings" in order to respect each another.

"The need was always there for that, and 9/11 only accelerated the process. We didn't always see the need. We live in a neighborhood, we are part of a neighborhood. Therefore, we need to act like neighbors. There can be no 'my way or the highway.' We can't do that now. Maybe we could a hundred years ago when we didn't know our neighbors, but even then it was wrong."

The Ahmeds tell some memorable stories about their Christian neighbors during their thirty years of living in Batavia. Like Marcia next door. Back when the Muslim congregation met in the Ahmeds' home for weekly prayers, Marcia unlocked the house every Friday for six weeks while the Ahmeds were visiting India. She prepared the prayer rugs, shoveled snow from the sidewalks, and kept an eye on the cars parked along the street. This story brings tears to Mazher's eyes because Marcia recently died from cancer. Mazher says that Marcia received all of the goodness from the prayers offered during those six weeks.

Then there was the elderly neighbor who accompanied the Ahmeds' daughter to school on grandparents' day since their daughter's own grandparents live in India. And the woman who translated the Friday sermons into sign language for a deaf Muslim man while sitting between him and the *khatib* (preacher) in the basement prayer room of Calvary Church.

Of course, not all of the Ahmeds' neighbors have shown them such Christian neighborliness. Still, they point out that "the bad neighbors make you appreciate the good ones," and most of their neighbors have been very good. Paraphrasing a saying of the Prophet Muhammad, Mahzer told us that if your neighbor goes hungry while you eat, you have committed a sin because you did not fulfill your duty as a neighbor. "The concept of sharing—if they are in need of your support, your help, you should be there—this concept is in all religions. Whether it is Christianity or Islam, you have this concept of being the neighbor. What constitutes a neighbor? Who is your neighbor?" Mahzer answered her own question: "Who is next door?"

For the Ahmeds, this makes the relationship between Calvary Church and Batavia Islamic Center especially poignant since it is neighbor helping neighbor across religious boundaries. "This was because of a human need," Mahzer explained. "They came from two different places, two different faiths, but they still worked it out. [The church] had a space they didn't use, and it was great of them that they thought, 'Well, these people do not have a space, so let them have that space.' They had this kindness and compassion in their heart."

Since 2002 Fr. Michael Rasicci has been rector of Calvary Church. We asked him about his approach to religious diversity, as well as his congregation's approach generally. He believes that Christians should share the Gospel, but "We always have to do it in a way that is respectful of others and their beliefs and not by approaching as some do, saying that unless you believe in Jesus Christ, believe in Jesus Christ in our way, you are lost. I don't think that that approach is really true, and I also don't believe it gets us very far. I think that ultimately God is the one that makes those judgments." In addition, Fr. Rasicci admits that sharing the Gospel through evangelizing or witnessing to others does not come easily to most Episcopalians. He says he would be "extremely pleased, although very surprised" were his congregation to engage in this kind of activity.

Father Rasicci draws upon the documents of the Second Vatican Council (Vatican II), the major Roman Catholic conference in the 1960s, especially the "Declaration on Religious Freedom," which stresses both respect for the world's religions and the church's duty to share the Gospel. "One must remember that, whatever the situation, God has already been there and that in some ways most of the world religions, if not all, share in parts of the truth that we would say, as Christians, we have the privilege to have in its fullness. People who are truly good people because of their religious affiliation and their living out of their faith are certainly going to be judged by God according to the criteria in their own religion."

Father Rasicci draws biblical guidance from the passage in John 10 where Jesus mentions his "other sheep." "There might be many flocks and more than one shepherd," Fr. Rasicci speculates, "and I can give that a wide interpretation, saying that Jesus died for all of humanity; he didn't just die for me. And that the redemption that Christ won for humanity is meant to be something that all people share. They have a relationship to God, and that still means, to me, they have the opportunity to live into that fullness of life that we have."

The Old Testament story of Abraham is particularly pertinent to the relationship between the three monotheistic religions that originated in the Middle East—Judaism, Christianity, and Islam. Rather than dwelling on the divergent views of Abraham, Fr. Rasicci prefers to invoke the genius of the Anglican tradition, which seeks God's larger perspective: "We call it 'inclusive' today—it used to be called 'comprehensive'—trying to see the whole picture and where people can fit into this whole picture of God's plan and the plan of salvation. Where these other religions fit into this, as opposed to how we can say who's in and who's out.... This is the way God would want us to be."

Father Rasicci summed up his congregation's approach to religious diversity in this way: "I would say our belief in God as the creator of all life moves us to take Christ's commandment to love seriously, and that includes people who differ from us in their approach to God. I think Christ, as our Lord, will judge us not on our theology but on how we loved."

Over the years, Calvary Episcopal Church has provided its members and the local community with numerous opportunities to learn about Islam. The Ahmeds often speak to the congregation and bring in Muslim guests. Many church members help out when the Muslims hold their annual *iftar* celebration (a dinner breaking the fast during the sacred month of Ramadan) at the church. Together, the church and the mosque have played an important role in the local response to the events of September 11, 2001. For instance, on the first anniversary of 9/11, they participated in an interfaith prayer service at a United Methodist church. Mazher Ahmed is not disappointed that several local churches chose not to participate on principle. She believes that some day all of the churches will come together for intergroup harmony. (See sidebar 4.1 for Mazher Ahmed's editorial on the first anniversary of 9/11.)

"They can do a whole lot," she explained to us, "more than the government can ever do. Because your daily life is connected with the church, not the government." She is hopeful about the future. "I am sure that one of these days we will all come together.... We will change the world and show that this little community of Batavia, this middle-class, Midwest town, can be an example to the world out there that we can coexist, that we can be happy, and that we can help each other in spite of our differences."

In another post-9/11 initiative, Batavia Islamic Center and Calvary Episcopal Church, in cooperation with the U.S. State Department's International Visitors Center of Chicago, hosted a series of panel discussions on Judaism, Christianity, and Islam, which featured delegations of international Muslim visitors from Europe, the Middle East, and Africa. The delegation from Africa was so astounded that a church would allow a Muslim congregation to worship in its facility that they took pictures of the church to show their fellow Muslims back home.

"That was so funny," says Mazher Ahmed. "They were speechless. They couldn't believe they were allowed to pray in a church."

In the early 1990s the Muslim congregation in Batavia opened a new mosque facility in Aurora, just to the south. However, the extra driving time was inconvenient for several members, so a group within the Muslim congregation eventually renewed their arrangement with Calvary Episcopal Church in Batavia. Besides, they had come to consider Calvary Church their "home" in many ways. The new Aurora mosque retained the congregation's original name, Fox Valley Muslim Community Center, while the Batavia group adopted the name Batavia Islamic Center.

According to our sources, little negative sentiment has been expressed within Calvary Church during its long relationship with Batavia Islamic Center, and most of that has had to do with mundane matters like forgetting to lock the building after an activity. Father Green recalls the concern that arose once over Islamic

SIDEBAR 4.1
Excerpt from "Killing Is Wrong, and It Doesn't
Matter Who Does It," by Mazher Ahmed, First
Anniversary of 9/11

All of a sudden at 8:46 A.M. Sept. 11 [2001] the peace of my
Midwest town, as well as the rest of my country, was shattered
when the first plane hit the World Trade Center. That moment
changed everything in our lives—we lost our innocence and
openness, which are synonymous to the American way of life.

These terrorists are not the true representation of Islam,
which teaches us to be human, kind, compassionate and love
our neighbors. It says in the Quran if you kill a person, you kill
humanity. It is not okay to kill innocents. Even when fighting a
war, you're not supposed to kill the children, women, and aged,
and you're not supposed to destroy farms. These are the rules
of engagement. What these people did was not an act of war. It
was an act of terror....

We have made bonds with churches. We are planning a
day-of-prayer event around September 11. I want to keep these
friendships and keep this bond we have so September 11 does
not happen again. I think knowledge brings you closer. Ignorance
breeds contempt. We as human beings are always afraid of the
unknown.

Source: *Daily Herald* (September 11, 2002), 19.

ritual ablutions. Muslims are required to wash various parts of the
body, including the feet, in preparation for prayer. When they used
a bathroom sink, some church members objected. An alternative
was arranged, and the Muslims were allowed access to the janitor's
closet, with its large tub and spigot. Like good neighbors, the two
groups worked things out to their mutual satisfaction.

In the aftermath of the events of September 11, 2001,
churches throughout the country reached out to local Muslim

communities. For instance, St. Thomas United Methodist Church in suburban Chicago held a joint service for peace with the mosque across the street a few days after 9/11. The two groups reunited the following year for a worship service and picnic. One lay leader of the church stated that this event was not a "one-shot deal." "They are going to be our neighbors," said Dave Thomas, invoking the key relationship discussed in this chapter. "We are planning interfaith dialogues. They are members of our community."

For More Information

Calvary Episcopal Church's contact information is 222 S. Batavia Avenue, Batavia, IL 60510; phone 630-879-3378; http://www.calvary-episcopal.org. Calvary is affiliated with the Episcopal Church USA, which has an Office of Ecumenical and Interfaith Relations (http://www.episcopalchurch.org/eir.htm). Various versions of the Anglican *Book of Common Prayer* can be found at http://anglicansonline.org/resources/bcp.html.

Documents of the Second Vatican Council, such as "Declaration on Religious Freedom" (*Dignitatis humanae*), are archived on the Vatican's Web site, http://www.vatican.va.

The Web site of the Batavia Islamic Center, http://www.bataviaislamiccenter.com/Batavia/Home.asp, features a photo gallery that gives a feel for the religious and social life of the Muslim members, including a Ramadan interfaith dinner. The Web site for the Council of Islamic Organizations of Greater Chicago, a local Muslim umbrella organization, is http://www.ciogc.org. For a readable scholarly treatment of Islam in the United States, see Jane I. Smith, *Islam in America* (New York: Columbia University Press, 1999).

The U.S. State Department operates international visitors centers in several major cities in the United States. The Web site for the Chicago center is http://www.ivcc.org.

Mazher Ahmed's essay, "Killing Is Wrong, and It Doesn't Matter Who Does It," appeared in a special section of the *Daily Herald,* a suburban Chicago newspaper (Sept. 11, 2002), 19.

The story of St. Thomas United Methodist Church discussed at the end of this chapter can be found in the online news archives of the Northern Illinois Conference of the United Methodist Church for October 2002, http://www.gbgm-umc.org/nillconf/umroct02. htm#101801. For another interesting relationship between a church and mosque, see the story of St. Paul's United Methodist Church and the Islamic Society of the East Bay, who built their facilities side by side in Fremont, California, excerpted from Diana Eck's *A New Religious America: How a "Christian" Country Has Now Become the World's Most Religiously Diverse Nation* (San Francisco: HarperSanFrancisco, 2001) at http://www.beliefnet. com/story/82/story_8210_1.html.

For Discussion

1. Calvary Episcopal Church has had a relationship with Batavia Islamic Center since 1987. Other churches, like St. Thomas United Methodist Church (featured at the end of this chapter), established relationships with nearby mosques in response to the events of September 11, 2001. Do you think these recent relationships will last very long? How important to long-term viability are the circumstances under which relationships between churches and mosques begin?

2. What role does serendipity play in the relationships between local churches and non-Christian groups? How important are the individuals involved? How would the relationship between Calvary Church and Batavia Islamic Center have evolved without the Ahmeds, Jim Hansen, or Calvary's rectors?

3. Evaluate the various motivations for hosting the Muslim congregation expressed by Calvary Church's leaders, such as treating non-Christians with respect. Recall Fr. Michael Rasicci's observation that evangelizing or witnessing to others does not come easily to

most Episcopalians. Do you think Calvary Church should do more along these lines?

4. Father Rasicci spoke of the genius of the Anglican tradition, which tries to see "the whole picture" from God's perspective, an "inclusive" or "comprehensive" understanding of how various groups fit into God's overall plan of salvation. How do you think Muslims fit into that plan?

5. Discuss the notion of neighborliness, so prominent in this chapter and expressed by both Christian and Muslim interviewees. What does it mean to show Christian neighborliness to non-Christians? Which acts of neighborliness in this chapter most impressed you?

6. What do you make of the fact that several Batavia churches declined to participate in the interfaith prayer service on the first anniversary of 9/11? Is Mazher Ahmed naïve to think that some day all of the churches will come together for intergroup harmony? Is she also naïve to think that "this little community of Batavia, this middle-class, Midwest town, can be an example to the world out there that we can coexist, that we can be happy, and that we can help each other in spite of our differences"?

7. The notion of "sacred space" is common in the world's religions, the idea that certain places are uniquely special or holy. Jim Hansen wondered whether Muslims would want to pray in Calvary Church, while the visiting African delegation expressed surprise that a church allows Muslims to do so. What do you think about religious groups sharing sacred space? Did it make a difference in the case presented in this chapter that the Muslims worship in the church basement rather than in the sanctuary?

8. Bible passages: Jesus mentions his "other sheep" in John 10:16. Father Rasicci summed up his congregation's approach to religious diversity by saying that they "take Christ's commandment to love seriously, and that includes people who differ from us in their approach to God." Christ's Great Commandment is found in Matthew 22:34–40.

FIVE

Struggling to Reach Out: St. Silas Lutheran Church

A YEAR HAD ELAPSED SINCE the September 11, 2001, attacks on the World Trade Center in New York City and the Pentagon in Washington, D.C. Pastor Jack Fischer thought it was time to address a palpable concern within the membership of St. Silas Lutheran Church,[1] a Missouri Synod congregation in suburban Chicago—anxiety over the unchurched in a new and unstable world. Pastor Jack prepared a sermon series that, in his words, would "anchor the general apologetic of their Christian faith." He sought as much to sharpen his people's understanding of their own Christian beliefs as to educate them about Islam. In the end he wished to equip them to witness for Christ to individual Muslims they might meet in their neighborhoods, workplaces, and elsewhere in daily life.

Pastor Jack titled the sermon series "Islam through the Eyes of Jesus," a clever reversal of the approach to Islam that explores Islamic perspectives on Christ and Christian beliefs, such as "Jesus through the Eyes of Islam." Yet Pastor Jack felt anything but clever in preparing a Christian critique of Islam. He confided to us later that he was daunted by the complexity of the topic and that his

---

1. At the church's request, St. Silas and the individual names in this chapter are pseudonyms.

bibliographic sources gave conflicting information. Moreover, as we shall see, he had an extended conversation with two Lutheran missionaries who themselves disagreed about key aspects of his opening sermon. "I grew a great deal during that series," Pastor Jack told us.

The worship service on the first Sunday established Christ as the starting and ending points for the series. The organ prelude included the hymn "All Hail the Power of Jesus' Name," while a congregational hymn concluded with the lines, "I love the name of Jesus / Immanuel, Christ, the Lord / Like fragrance on the breezes / His name abroad is poured." The lay leader prayed that God would remember the United States in its time of need and shared his personal burden for those who do not know Jesus as their Lord and Savior, including the vast number of Muslims worldwide.

Pastor Jack introduced his sermon with a brief prayer asking God to help Christians find bridges to walk across in order to witness to Muslims about Jesus Christ. He offered disclaimers for the sermon series by admitting no expertise in Islam and granting his listeners permission to disagree with him. He said he hoped to avoid oversimplifying Islam, but he also made it clear that he cared little for political correctness.

Two key points stood out in this opening sermon of the series. First, Pastor Jack distinguished the God of Christianity from the god of Islam. "Allah is their god," he said. This is not a matter of mere semantics. "Allah" is not simply the Arabic name for the God worshiped by Christians. These are two completely different gods, only one of which is the true God.

Second, Pastor Jack contrasted the two religions in uncompromising terms. Several times he characterized Islam as a "hostile" religion whose goal is that "everyone submit to Allah." He cited 1 Timothy 2:1–6 in order to contrast the peace-loving nature of Christianity with the violent nature of Islam. "Islam evangelizes with the sword," he explained, whereas "Christianity evangelizes with a message, with the Gospel." Islam's founder, Muhammad, sowed seeds of deep hatred for Jews and Christians, whom he considered infidels, and Islam's scripture, the Qur'an, instructs Muslims to fight infidels. "Jesus shed his own blood to advance the Kingdom of God among us here on earth," Pastor Jack asserted,

while "Muhammad shed the blood of others to advance the kingdom of Allah, the Islamic kingdom here on earth." This is why Islam
soon came to be called "the religion of the sword." He also cited
the words of one historian: "Islam is intrinsically an intolerant,
violent religion." Pastor Jack acknowledged contradictory voices
within contemporary Islam on this matter, with modernist Muslims
emphasizing the peaceful passages of the Qur'an. Nonetheless, he
said, the fundamentalist Muslim voice dominates Islam today.

Pastor Jack closed with the following point, which anticipated
the main topic of the second sermon in the series: "Islam claims
to have the truth. Christianity claims to have the truth. Different
truths. Now, if you look at it objectively, theoretically we could
both be wrong.... But we could not both be right."

Listening to Pastor Jack's opening sermon with great interest
was Rev. Wilton DeMast. Not only did Wilt have more than thirty
years of experience in Lutheran missionary work in Muslim lands,
but he had also been asked by Pastor Jack to lead an adult discussion session on Islam in conjunction with the sermon series. Wilt
was concerned about the content of this first sermon.

"I was a bit disappointed at what [Pastor Jack] presented,"
Wilt wrote the next day in an extended e-mail to a former missionary colleague who had taught Wilt a great deal about Islam.
"After the service someone asked me what I thought of the sermon. One part of me said to lie, and the other said tell the truth.
So I told the truth gently. I said the sermon was a bit inflamma-
tory. It would make the members tend to hate Muslims. I really
don't think this is the way to go." Wilt thought he should talk to
Pastor Jack before the adult discussion class. He did not wish to
appear to subvert the pastor's authority in the way he intended
to present Islam to the group.

Wilt met with Pastor Jack later that week, along with a missionary associate. Wilt shared his concerns, as he described to us in
an interview. First of all, Wilt believed Pastor Jack had gone "way
too far" in focusing on the violent side of Islam. This was unfair
without a comparable discussion of the violent side of Christianity,
like the Crusades, certain racist groups in the United States, and
South African apartheid. It is very dangerous to broadly character-
ize Islam as a violent religion, Wilt told us. Not all Muslims are

suicide bombers and terrorists. Christians need to know about the average, hard-working Muslim majority.

Second, Wilt challenged Pastor Jack's contention that Allah and the Christian God are different gods. Wilt sees them as the same God—Muslims simply take the wrong approach and end up with a different understanding of God. To say that Allah is a different God becomes very problematic in that it raises questions about the Jews and their understanding of God. Moreover, to say that Allah is a different God is problematic when dealing with Arab converts to Christianity since "Allah" is the Arabic word for "God." As Wilt put it, drawing upon his linguistic training as a missionary, "There can't be two Allahs, Allah[1] of the Muslims and Allah[2] of the Christians."

Wilt's missionary colleague at the meeting found this latter point unacceptable and sided with Pastor Jack that Allah cannot possibly be the God that Christians worship. Nonetheless, Wilt remained adamant and criticized the false logic of the argument that, because Muslims understand God differently, they therefore worship a different God. If Christians are ever going to witness to Muslims effectively, Wilt maintained, they must enter into dialogue with them from the premise that both faiths worship the same God. He cited the approach of Bible translators working with the language of the Moba people in West Africa, who use the Moba word for God, *yennu,* to translate the Greek word for God in the New Testament, *theos.* Wilt finds hints of Christian doctrine in Moba myths, which can provide an entrée for conversation with potential Moba converts. Like the Mobas' understanding of *yennu,* Islam's understanding of Allah contains dim perceptions of the one true God as fully revealed in Christianity. (See sidebar 5.1 for the views of Martin Luther, the founder of the Lutheran branch of Protestant Christianity.)

Coming away from this debate with Pastor Jack and his missionary colleague, Wilt decided to avoid the topic of Allah with his discussion group and to present instead a kind of "Islam 101" overview of other key topics, such as the Qur'an and Islamic groups. He also shared personal anecdotes from his missionary work among Muslims. To the group, he summarized the objective for the session in this way: "Why do this study on Islam? So we can understand where they [Muslims] are coming from and be able to

SIDEBAR 5.1
Excerpt from Martin Luther's *Large Catechism*, 1529

These articles of the Creed, therefore, divide and separate us Christians from all other people upon earth. For all outside of Christianity, whether heathen, Turks, Jews, or false Christians and hypocrites, although they believe in, and worship, only one true God, yet know not what His mind towards them is, and cannot expect any love or blessing from Him; therefore they abide in eternal wrath and damnation. For they have not the Lord Christ, and, besides, are not illumined and favored by any gifts of the Holy Ghost.

Source: *Large Catechism*, "The Apostles' Creed," 66 (http://www.bookofconcord.org/largecatechism/4_creed.html).

witness about Christ to them effectively." Clearly, Wilt and Pastor Jack agreed on the goal of saving Muslims' souls. They differed, however, on the proper portrayal of Islam and the best strategy in approaching Muslims.

Ted Rudriger also took a keen interest in Pastor Jack's opening sermon in the series on Islam. Ted is on staff at St. Silas Church, and his primary responsibility is the integration of new members into the congregation. In the late 1960s and early 1970s he served as a language consultant for missionary work in a part of Nigeria surrounded by Muslim territory. The Biafran civil war broke out during that period, which included a brutal massacre of a tribal group by ethnic Muslims. Ted is quick to point out that the massacre was not attributable to Islam.

During the worship service, Ted was the lay leader who shared his personal burden for the unsaved masses of the world, especially Muslims. As he and Wilt DeMast compared notes after the service, both raised their eyebrows at Pastor Jack's tone and approach in the sermon. Ted believed at the time that the sermon might have "inflamed" some of the people in the audience and that Pastor Jack had been less tactful than he himself would have been. Upon further reflection, however, Ted was pleased with Pastor Jack's forcefulness. Thankfully, in Ted's view, this would not be another soft-pedaling of Islam like those he had often heard following 9/11. (For a controversial response to 9/11 by a Missouri Synod official, see sidebar 5.2.)

We asked Ted whether Pastor Jack's portrayal of Islam matched his own experience with Muslims in Nigeria. He found it "fairly accurate." He acknowledged that some members of the congregation were upset by the grotesque and violent aspects of the sermon, but that is the reality of Islam, in Ted's judgment. Some Muslims may claim they are a peace-loving people, he told us, but you do not have to dig very far into the Qur'an to see the opposite. He granted that some Muslim groups may be less violent than others, but the bottom line is that they all believe "Islam will prevail worldwide." Liberal segments of the Muslim community lull people to sleep by claiming, "We're not dangerous." Yet they have the same laws, the same Qur'an, and the same goal as all Muslims.

SIDEBAR 5.2
Controversy over "A Prayer for America"

As president of the Lutheran Church–Missouri Synod's Atlantic District and pastor of a Brooklyn church, Rev. David Benke participated in "A Prayer for America," a public event held at Yankee Stadium just days after September 11, 2001. His presence on the program with Christian and non-Christian leaders provoked a controversy within the denomination, primarily over whether Rev. Benke had violated denominational bans on "unionism" (with other Christians) and "syncretism" (with non-Christians) in worship. In June of 2002 Rev. Benke was suspended from his ministerial and administrative duties but reinstated by a denominational dispute panel the following May.

As to the debate over Allah, Ted explained: "The cutting edge is Jesus Christ. The difference between Jehovah God and Allah is Jesus Christ." These are not the same God, he said emphatically, and we are not all going to the same place eternally.

The sermon series "Islam through the Eyes of Jesus" continued for four more Sundays at St. Silas Church. In the second install-ment, titled "Why Can't We All Get Along?" Pastor Jack picked up where he had concluded the first sermon, with the issue of competing religious truth claims. Modern culture today believes that knowledge of God is a matter of personal taste and prefer-ence, Pastor Jack explained, that truth is relative, that there are no "right" answers, and that all religions are simply different paths to the same ultimate goal. But this is not the Christian view. Pastor Jack shared his surprise at the conversations he so often hears around the casket at funeral visitations, to the effect that "they're in a better place now." This may or may not be the case, Pastor Jack corrected. If they did not have faith in Jesus Christ, "they're in a worse place now," he said.

Islam and Christianity differ in fundamental ways, Pastor Jack asserted. Islam teaches that one is saved by pleasing Allah with good deeds, whereas Christianity teaches that salvation is a gift of God's grace through Jesus Christ. Islam claims that Allah is God and that Muhammad is God's prophet, whereas Christianity claims that Jesus is the way, the truth, and the life. Islam is based on the Qur'an, Christianity on the Bible. These are contradictory claims. Both religions could be wrong, Pastor Jack conceded. However, Christians know the truth through the Bible. "And the Bible is not an opinion," Pastor Jack proclaimed.

At one point in this second sermon, perhaps in consideration of his conversation with Wilt DeMast a few days before, Pastor Jack noted the Crusades as a dark chapter in Christian history and called them an "evil thing," even "a Christian jihad" (in the sense of a "holy war"). He admitted that there is no difference between the Christian Crusaders of the Middle Ages and today's Muslim terrorists. Even though the Crusades occurred more than a thou-sand years ago, Pastor Jack explained, and "we had no part of that," Christians cannot justify them in any way.

In the third sermon of the series, Pastor Jack elaborated on his contention that Islam and Christianity hold incompatible views of salvation. At its core, Islam believes that people must follow Allah's laws in order to escape the flames of hell. Paradise, or heaven, is a distant hope in Islam, which believes that most people will not reach it. Christianity, in contrast, is about having a relationship with God through Jesus Christ, not about following divine laws. The Ten Commandments, for instance, are not rules for getting into heaven but rather guideposts of good living in response to God's salvation. Islam says that if you do not measure up, Allah will throw you into the fires of hell. Christians escape the fires of hell through Jesus, not by trying to measure up. Pastor Jack ended this sermon with a thought that had been troubling him: Could it be that Muslims are more motivated to live good lives out of their fear of hell than Christians—who will escape hell—are motivated to live good lives in gratitude for God's saving love?

Pastor Jack was absent for the fourth Sunday of the series, but the topic was continued with a personal testimony from a Pakistani Christian woman who was raised in the United Arab Emirates and attended a professional school in Pakistan, both predominantly Muslim countries. She said she appreciated Pastor Jack's sermons because she now understood the differences between Islam and Christianity, and she thanked God that she was a member of the "beautiful religion" of Christianity. Muslims had treated her like an infidel when she was growing up and showered her with epithets too embarrassing to repeat in church. For fear of persecution, her parents warned her not to compare the two religions or witness to the truth of Christianity. Muslims are highly intolerant, she asserted. As to the claim by many American Muslims that Islam is a religion of peace, she thinks they are simply saying such things in order to avoid deportation.

Pastor Jack opened the sermon series finale with a question-and-answer exercise with the congregation. Question: "Do you believe that God loves Muslim people?" The congregation gave a consensus "Yes," which Pastor Jack confirmed. Question: "Do you think that Muslims believe that Allah loves them?" The congregation was unsure here, but Pastor Jack explained that the answer is "No." He elaborated: "Muslims believe that Allah is all powerful, he is great, he's in charge of everything, but he's remote, he's distant, there's no personal relationship with him, and there's no love, there's only fear of him. So Muslims live being afraid that Allah will eventually send them to hell to be punished because their life was not lived good enough." Ironically, Pastor Jack suggested, the god that Muslims have created does not even love them, while the God they do not know, the God that Christians know in Jesus Christ, does. This leads to the most important point of the entire sermon series, he continued: "If Jesus Christ loves Muslims, then we should love Muslims." Pastor Jack illustrated this point with stories of Christians showing love to Muslim neighbors and acquaintances, thereby fulfilling Jesus' injunction to "let your light shine before men, that they may see your good deeds and praise your Father in heaven" (Matthew 5:16, as printed in the worship bulletin).

It is difficult to assess the impact of this sermon series on the members of St. Silas Lutheran Church. Pastor Jack received mostly positive direct comments, such as thanking him for giving the battle cry for the army of good and for informing the congregation about current world events. Other than the disagreement with Wilt DeMast, Pastor Jack received negative direct comments from only two people. One, who had received multicultural sensitivity training in the armed forces, took exception to some of Pastor Jack's characterizations of Islam. The other, a father who had heard about the series secondhand, almost pulled his child out of the church's preschool over it. He blamed all Muslims for the September 11 attacks and believed that the United States should never have let Muslim immigrants into the country. He wanted nothing to do with the notion that Christians ought to love Muslims. Perhaps most satisfying to Pastor Jack was the fact that the principals identified in this chapter maintained their collegiality throughout the sermon series despite their differences of opinion.

To date, St. Silas Church has not made religious diversity a programming priority. The sermon series on Islam was the church's most systematic and intentional effort ever on this issue. A far more central concern for this church has been ethnic diversity among Christians. A predominantly German American congregation for most of its history (est. 1857), St. Silas established a dual site ministry in the 1980s that included an Hispanic Lutheran mission congregation drawn largely from the changing neighborhood around the church's original site. The relationship between the two congregations was strained at times (St. Silas sold the property to the Hispanic church in 2005), but it forced the white members of St. Silas to examine the relative claims of cultural identity and the Gospel. Ted Rudriger, who takes an appreciative approach to Christianity's varied ethnic expressions, explained that "Cultural differences are good, but without Christ, we are not doing anyone a favor by supporting cultural differences. We need to find a way to accommodate culture, but with Christ as a part of it. Culture can be preserved, but we all need the Savior, Jesus Christ." When we asked Ted whether the congregation's multicultural experience offered transferable skills with regard to Muslims and other non-Christians, he responded without hesitation: "Very definitely. What we learn as a congregation in terms of worldview, leadership, and sensitivity to cultural differences is invaluable. But we need to stand firm as a congregation, as a carrier of the Christian faith. Scripture is very clear about how salvation is attained."

Wilt DeMast agreed. Nonetheless, he admitted that it has not been easy for St. Silas Church. Wilt summarized the congregation's attempts to carry the Gospel message across ethnic and religious boundaries with the phrase that serves as this chapter's title: Struggling to Reach Out.

For More Information

For the Lutheran Church–Missouri Synod's perspective on Islam, see the document produced by the denomination's Commission on Theology and Church Relations, "Islam," at http://www.lcms.org/graphics/assets/media/CTCR/Islam%201207.pdf. For denominational coverage of the controversy over Rev. David Benke's participation in "A Prayer for America" in New York City, go to http://www.lcms.org and type the word "Benke" into the search function. For other Lutheran perspectives on Islam and Muslims see "Windows for Understanding: Jewish-Muslim-Lutheran Relations," downloadable from the Web site of the Evangelical Lutheran Church in America's office of Ecumenical and Inter-Religious Relations (http://archive.elca.org/ecumenical/interreligious/windows.html), and Sigvard von Sicard and Ingo Wulfhorst, eds., "Dialogue and Beyond: Christians and Muslims Together on the Way" (Geneva: Lutheran World Federation, 2003; http://www.lutheranworld.org).

People of the Book Lutheran Outreach (POBLO) is a Lutheran mission initiative toward Muslims. For stories about POBLO, go to the Lutheran Church–Missouri Synod's Web site, http://www.lcms.org, and type the word "POBLO" into the search function.

The Zwemer Center for Muslim Studies conducts research on Islam and trains Christians to evangelize Muslims. Formerly located on the campus of Concordia Theological Seminary (Fort Wayne, Indiana), a Lutheran Church–Missouri Synod seminary, it is now located at Columbia International University, Columbia, South Carolina. The Zwemer Center's Web site is http://www.ciu.edu/seminary/muslimstudies.

In preparing his sermon series, Pastor Jack Fischer considered the following book the most helpful source on Islam: Ergun Mehmet Caner and Emir Fethi Caner, *Unveiling Islam: An Insider's Look at Muslim Life and Beliefs* (Grand Rapids, Mich.: Kregel, 2002). For another treatment of Islam see R. Marston Speight, *God Is One: The Way of Islam,* 2d ed. (New York: Friendship, 2001). For a historical overview of relations between the world's two largest religions see Hugh Goddard, *A History of Christian-Muslim Relations* (Chicago: New Amsterdam Books, 2000).

The Muslim Web site http://www.islamanswers.net is recommended by missionary Wilt DeMast. Also, see http://www.islamic-ity.com and the Web site of the Islamic Society of North America, http://www.isna.net.

For Discussion

1. Pastor Jack Fischer and missionary Wilt DeMast differed in their starting points in evangelizing Muslims, Pastor Jack stressing the

contrasts between Christianity and Islam, Wilt using commonalities as the entrée to conversation. Which approach do you think is a more effective evangelization strategy?

2. Do Muslims and Christians pray to the same God? In a survey of evangelical Christian leaders in the United States, nearly 80 percent said no; nearly 90 percent believed it is very important to insist on the truth of the Gospel when interacting with Muslims (http://www.beliefnet.com/story/124/story_12447_1.html). What are the implications of these views for Christian relations with Muslims and other non-Christians?

3. Do you think Pastor Jack gave an accurate portrayal of Islam and Muslims in his sermon series? Do you think others in this chapter did? What is an "accurate portrayal" of Islam and Muslims? How do you explain the fact that Pastor Jack's bibliographic sources gave conflicting information?

4. Pastor Jack told us that one of his greatest lessons from the sermon series was "If Jesus loves Muslims, then I probably should also." How would Jesus show love toward Muslims today? Do you agree with the individuals in this chapter that the most important way of showing love to non-Christians is to bring them into a saving relationship with Jesus Christ?

5. Can you distinguish the core claims of the Gospel from cultural expressions of Christianity in your congregation? Do you agree with Ted Rudriger that appreciation for cultural variations within Christianity and sensitivity in approaching adherents of non-Christian religions go hand in hand?

6. Bible passages: Missionary Wilt DeMast draws inspiration from Ephesians 2:1–10, which he says lays out God's whole plan of salvation through grace. Jesus' injunction to "let your light shine before men, that they may see your good deeds and praise your Father in heaven" (Matthew 5:16) was printed in a worship bulletin for Pastor Jack Fischer's sermon series on Islam.

SIX

Gathering around the Table of Fellowship: Lake Street Church

THE WORSHIP SERVICE ON SUNDAY, October 6, 2002, began with an invocation by an Aztec dance group asking for a blessing from the four directions of the earth. One after another, local representatives of Hinduism, Buddhism, Judaism, Islam, and other religious traditions shared something appropriate to the interfaith theme of the service, "Building Community: Repairing the World Together." A Hindu swami intoned the sacred Sanskrit syllable Om, Buddhist monks chanted ancient Pali scriptures, a Muslim imam recited passages from the Qur'an, and an adherent of Sant Mat (a spiritual tradition with historical roots in northwest India) offered a guided meditation on the sources of inner peace and care for others. Christian elements were interspersed throughout the service, such as the congregational hymn "Joyful, Joyful, We Adore Thee" and the choir's anthem, "Prayer of St. Francis." The pastor of the church, Rev. Robert Thompson, closed the service by leading the people in a commitment to peace. The interfaith movement is "bubbling up" all over the world, he proclaimed approvingly. (See sidebar 6.1 for a list of the groups who participated in this interfaith service.)

This annual interfaith worship service epitomizes the approach to religious diversity at Lake Street Church of Evanston, Illinois, just north of Chicago. In turn, Lake Street Church and its pastor

---

SIDEBAR 6.1
Groups Participating in Worldwide Community Sunday Service, Lake Street Church, October 6, 2002

Beth Emet, the Free Synagogue (Judaism), http://www.bethemet.org

Buddhist Council of the Midwest (Buddhism), http://www.buddhistcouncilmidwest.org

Chinmaya Mission Chicago (Hinduism), http://www.chinmaya-chicago.org

Grupo Ehécatl (Aztec indigenous spirituality) (no Web site)

Jain Society of Metropolitan Chicago (Jainism), http://www.jsmconline.org

Muslim Community Center (Islam), http://www.mcchicago.org

Nartan School of Dance (classical dance tradition in India) (no Web site)

Pachamama Alliance (indigenous eco-religion), http://www.pachamama.org

Science of Spirituality (Sant Mat), http://www.sos.org

Sikh Religious Society of Chicago (Sikh faith), http://www.srschicago.com

Soundvision Foundation (Islam), http://www.soundvision.com

---

epitomize key aspects of the modern interfaith movement, as well as key challenges for its Christian participants.

Lake Street Church held its first interfaith service in 1996 on World Wide Communion Sunday, an ecumenical Protestant observance held annually on the first Sunday in October. The idea of opening the Christian ritual of Communion to non-Christian participants strikes some as daring, others as inappropriate and perhaps even blasphemous. The photo on Rev. Thompson's office wall, which shows Buddhist monks blessing the Communion elements at one of these services, is a conversation piece, to put it mildly.

The *Chicago Sun-Times* reported on the 1998 service at Lake Street Church in an article titled "Minister Sets Communion Table for All," citing Rev. Thompson's justification for the event. In explanation, Rev. Thompson wondered how Christians could exclude non-Christians from experiencing Christ's presence in the celebration of Communion. "That is a direct contradiction of what we see in Jesus, who was present with everybody, regardless of their standing in society," he asserted before continuing: "My responsibility is to cultivate an atmosphere that celebrates a kind of respect for everyone's tradition. And the way I know how to do that is to take down barriers that existed in the past."

We interviewed Rev. Thompson not long after the 2002 interfaith service described earlier. He has since changed the name to Worldwide Community Sunday, but the philosophy behind the event remains the same. Lake Street Church does not hold to any mindset that would distinguish between Christians and non-Christians, Rev. Thompson explained. At Lake Street Church, religious boundaries are loosely drawn, and the congregation is "intentionally ambiguous" about its own identity. The more tightly drawn the boundaries, the more exclusive the congregation, Rev. Thompson observed.

Lake Street Church (est. 1858) is officially affiliated with the American Baptist Churches USA denomination but recently changed its name from First Baptist Church in order to avoid scaring away people for whom the word "Baptist" carries negative connotations. The congregation has formed a committee to explore possible new affiliations, such as the Unitarian Universalist Association, the United Church of Christ, the Religious Society of Friends (the Quakers), the Association of Unity Churches, or even a Buddhist connection of some kind, which makes sense considering the congregation's strong ties to local Buddhist groups (see later discussion). Whatever direction they take, Rev. Thompson feels that his congregation's spiritual vitality requires "a larger vessel" than the American Baptists provide.

Moreover, Rev. Thompson sees the Worldwide Community Sunday celebration as a way to be as "radically inclusive" as Jesus was in his own table fellowship. Jesus ate and drank with everyone, creating a scandalous feast under the banner of the Kingdom of God, welcoming those whom others would exclude from the kingdom. The church should be about relationships, Rev. Thompson asserted. "It's more important to be related than right."

He offered another metaphor for the church's relationship to a diverse religious world: Truth is like a precious jewel. Christians see some of the jewel's facets from their particular vantage point and depending on the light available to them. Adherents of other religions see other facets with their lights. The more collective light we shed on the jewel, the more truth we can all apprehend, he believes.

When we interviewed him, Rev. Thompson was chair of the board of trustees of the Council for a Parliament of the World's Religions, a major interfaith organization headquartered in Chicago (see the introduction to this book). A nun from the Brahma Kumaris spiritual group had nominated him to the board a few years earlier, but when he was asked to take over the chair, his first thought was that they needed a woman or a person of color. "They don't need another white, Christian guy," he recalled saying to himself. Upon reflection, however, he was happy to take the position since it continued and extended the interfaith work he had been involved with for several years, including that at a local homeless shelter.

In a sense, Lake Street Church is a miniature parliament of religions in that it provides a venue for dialogue and cooperation among a variety of local religious groups. The church has relationships with a Reform Jewish synagogue, a Baha'i spiritual assembly, a Sufi prayer group that meets at a well-known Islamic bookstore in Chicago, and a Sunni Islamic day school in an adjacent suburb with which the congregation is trying to organize a joint children's playgroup.

Perhaps the strongest connection is that with local Buddhists, including several meditation centers in the Evanston area. When Sakyong Mipham Rinpoche, son of Shambhala International's founder, Chogyam Trungpa Rinpoche, came to Chicago for a series of talks in 2003, he packed the sanctuary at Lake Street Church for a lecture on meditation in the Tibetan Buddhist tradition. The

SIDEBAR 6.2
Lake Street Church Hosts International Visakha

The Buddhist Council of the Midwest has sponsored an annual international Visakha celebration since the 1980s. Visakha commemorates the birth, enlightenment, and final passing away of Buddhism's founder and has become the setting for inter-Buddhist and interfaith activities across the United States.

When Lake Street Church hosts an international Visakha festival, the Buddhist Council of the Midwest receives queries: Why hold such a significant Buddhist celebration at a Christian church instead of a Buddhist temple or meditation center? Adequate parking is one advantage of the church, but that's not the whole story.

We attended a meeting of the Buddhist Council of the Midwest at which the topic came up for discussion. When someone floated the idea of holding future international Visakhas at a public venue like a high school, college, or civic center, the president objected: "We want someplace that has spirituality."

church regularly supports the work of Tibet Center, a local cultural organization with close ties to the Dalai Lama. The Buddhist Council of the Midwest, a regional umbrella group that represents dozens of Buddhist temples and meditation centers, has often held its annual international Visakha celebration at Lake Street Church (see sidebar 6.2). Heartland Sangha, a group that combines the Zen and Jodo Shinshu Buddhist traditions, has held its services at Lake Street Church for several years. The church also cosponsors an annual weekend seminar called "Living Buddha/Living Christ" with Lakeside Buddha Sangha, a Buddhist center that follows the teachings of the well-known Vietnamese Zen teacher Thich Nhat Hanh.

Several members of the church, including Lise (pronounced "Lisa") Jacobson, self-identify as Buddhists. After attending the international Visakha celebration at the church in 1999, she joined both Lakeside Buddha Sangha and Lake Street Church. When we interviewed her, she was serving as cochair of the church's interfaith committee. She calls Rev. Thompson the "guiding light" of the congregation's philosophy and interfaith activities, someone who possesses an almost "mystical" understanding of how individuals approach the divine. However, the church is not merely an extension of its pastor in these matters, Lise clarified. There is a hunger for understanding at Lake Street Church, she explained, and much of the programming that addresses non-Christian religions comes from the members themselves. Speaking for the interfaith committee, she said, "We just try to give people what they want."

Lise lightheartedly offered the phrase "chaotic exploration" to sum up Lake Street Church's approach to religious diversity. "There is so much going on," she elaborated, "so many different opinions. The church supports the diverse personal journeys of its members. We don't require that everyone take the same journey. We manage to support many different journeys." She attends Lake Street Church because she has Christian roots that she reveres despite having had "issues" while growing up. "It had nothing to do with Christ," she explained, "but the church." She said she now has an attachment to both the Christ and the Buddha. "Are they gods?" she asked. "No. Do I worship them? No. If the Christian police stopped me and asked if Jesus Christ is my Lord and Savior, I'm in trouble." But Lake Street Church has no Christian police, she told us.

Lise confessed to us that she acted a bit "ornery" at the last Worldwide Community Sunday service. She stood up twice when the leaders asked people to identify their religion, once as a Christian, next as a Buddhist. "If there were a census, I couldn't pick one," she explained. Then she reflected on the role of community in religious identities. She said she had never thought about community until the last few years, but "people need community." She is thankful to have two religious communities supporting her in her spiritual path. "We should stop romanticizing individualism."

Lake Street Church offers an array of spiritual options for inquiring individuals, all within the context of a supportive community.

"Spiritual seekers, regardless of racial, sexual, or religious orienta-
tions, are all welcome!" proclaims a church brochure, which also
notes that more than sixteen religious traditions are represented
in the congregation. For inquirers potentially turned off by the
church's Baptist affiliation, the brochure clarifies:

> Lake Street Church intentionally seeks to embody the best of
> the free-church tradition by encouraging individuals to forge
> a spiritual path based upon the intuitive wisdom of their own
> experience. We seek therefore to support individuals in their
> uniquely personal spiritual quests. Our spiritual community is
> not held together by belief in a particular doctrine but by the
> shared experience of our innate connection in and through the
> Divine.

A quotation from Phil Jenks, a World Council of Churches official
and an American Baptist, sums up Lake Street Church's understanding of "church": "When a group of people representing a variety of denominations, traditions, interpretations, and convictions
stand arm in arm prayerfully, God is in the center. Differences are
understood. Similarities are softly evident. Community happens.
The church has become."

At the time of our research, in addition to the usual Christian
programming one would expect of any church, Lake Street Church
offered the following programs and activities (the first three have
already been discussed): Worldwide Community Sunday, meditation lecture by Sakyong Mipham Rinpoche, Living Buddha/
Living Christ seminar, A-Little-Bit-of-Tibet (program on Tibetan
culture and religion), Awakening Our Cosmic Selves (workshop
on Buddhist meditation), Meditation Satsang (series on Hindu
meditation), the Yoga Studio, Light of the Moon Society (women's
spirituality group), Be-a-Muslim-for-Half-a-Day, and Bhagavad
Gita Discussion Group. We attended two sessions of the Bhagavad
Gita group, which meets during the adult Sunday school hour.

The group uses the three-volume commentary *The Bhagavad
Gita for Daily Living,* by Sri Eknath Easwaran, as a guide to understanding this Hindu scripture, as well as a catalyst for open discussion about a range of topics. In our first visit, the group considered

two passages from the Gita. The first passage reads as follows: "The spiritually minded, who eat in the spirit of service, are freed from all their sins; but the selfish, who prepare food for their own satisfaction, eat sin." Discussion centered around various spiritual paths, and one person drew a connection between the Gita passage and the Buddha's experimentation with ascetic fasting, which the Buddha eventually abandoned since that lifestyle could not lead to enlightenment. The group also engaged in a lively debate about the spiritual merits of vegetarianism. Some decried the hypocrisy of being a vegetarian while remaining violent in other ways through thought, word, or deed. A couple of people shared their personal struggles with cravings for various kinds of food that may be spiritually impure.

The second passage from the Gita continued the food theme: "Living creatures are nourished by food, and food is nourished by the rain; this rain is the water of life that comes from selfless action, worship, and service." Here the discussion focused on interior change and how it might alter the world. A spiritual ripple effect spreads outward from oneself to those immediately around one to the whole world. Separateness is an illusion; we influence each other and all things.

The conversation during this session made no reference to anything specifically Christian. Drawing connections between the Bhagavad Gita and the Bible or between Hinduism and Christianity is not required of the class. The conversation during the second session we visited did make a few such connections, however. For instance, the group compared the Christian notion of being "born again" with the "twice-born" status of Hindu Brahmins, the spiritual leaders of Hinduism. Also, the group agreed that the Hindu story of the god Krishna filling his flute with divine love and joy dovetailed nicely with 1 Corinthians 13, where the apostle Paul likens tongue speaking without love to the sound of noisy instruments.

We interviewed Al Kost, who led the Bhagavad Gita discussion group. Al was raised Jewish but now considers himself primarily a follower of Sri Eknath Easwaran, a spiritual teacher from south India and author of the Gita commentary used by the group. For Al, "Jesus was a messenger, not the message, but people are confused." Christians today have lost sight of Jesus' basic message of "loving thy neighbor" and have become too caught up in the Bible and supposedly correct practices. Christians should not respond to religious diversity by proselytizing. Rather, they should welcome diversity into their churches, as Lake Street Church does and as Jesus welcomed the variety around him in love. "God is love," Al offered. "If we love each other, it's all going to be fine. Though we have our share of problems, we try to be a loving community."

In Al's opinion, the most important issue facing Lake Street Church is how to embrace conservative Christians in love. The church has had far less success in reaching out to other churches than to non-Christian groups, and some of its own members sometimes feel uncomfortable with the extensive non-Christian programming at the church. We asked the moderator of the church, Patricia Ashbrook, for her thoughts on this issue.

Pat joined Lake Street Church in 1983. She describes herself as both a "traditional Baptist" and a "progressive Baptist" whose husband, father, uncle, and brother were all Baptist ministers. Nonetheless, she made sure we understood: "I don't like the Southern Baptists," who are far too conservative for her tastes. She believes strongly in the fundamental Baptist principles of individual freedom of belief and congregational autonomy, which Lake Street Church represents. She confessed that she does not always feel spiritually fed at Lake Street Church because she prefers more traditional expressions of Christianity, but the typical Sunday morning worship experience still "holds together" well enough as a Protestant service in her estimation. However, if the church ever swung completely away from Christianity, she told us, "I couldn't stay."

Pat described Lake Street Church as "inclusive, almost to an extreme." The congregation welcomes diversity in religious beliefs, sexual lifestyles, and racial/ethnic identities (although it is a predominantly white congregation), but it still manages to maintain a healthy equilibrium. "We have tensions," she admitted, "but we're able to deal with them." The variety is "like yeast—it brings life to the church. I don't always agree with the views, but it feels very good for us." She illustrated her point by referring to the church's heavy emphasis on Buddhism. She loves a lot of Buddhist sayings and recognizes that Buddhist meditation might be a centering influence for many members (her late husband meditated). "But it's not for me. I center myself in different ways," she said. She thinks congregational affiliation with a Buddhist group does not make sense. "We must be open and understanding of different faiths, but we can still be grounded in Christianity."

When we asked Rev. Thompson whether he sensed any serious disagreements within the congregation over its interfaith inclusiveness, he gave us a look familiar to anyone who knows churches and their propensity for divisiveness on any number of issues. "It's a church," he said simply. He acknowledged a minority but persistent refrain of discomfort within the membership, usually articulated in the question "Are we still a Christian church?" However, he asserted, "I really think what we're doing represents the future of liberal Protestantism. We've got to fulfill the promise of diversity. Spiritual imperialism creates a world of greater conflict. We don't need more monologue; we need dialogue."

For More Information

Lake Street Church's contact information is 607 Lake Street, Evanston, IL 60201; phone 847-864-2181; http://www.lakestreet. org. The congregation is currently affiliated with the American Baptist Churches USA denomination (http://www.abc-usa.org) but is considering several alternative affiliations, including the Buddhist Council of the Midwest (http://www.buddhistcouncil-midwest.org) given the congregation's strong relationship with local Buddhists. For a readable scholarly treatment of Buddhism in the United States see Richard Hughes Seager, *Buddhism in America* (New York: Columbia University Press, 1999). For information about local Buddhist councils, including the Buddhist Council of the Midwest, see my essay "Local Inter-Buddhist Associations in North America" in *American Buddhism: Methods and Findings in Recent Scholarship,* ed. Duncan Ryuken Williams and Christopher S. Queen (London: Curzon, 1999), 117–142.

World Communion Sunday, formerly called World Wide Communion Sunday, originated in Presbyterian circles in 1936 but is observed by a number of Protestant denominations today. Participating denominations and congregations share the Eucharist or Communion as a sign of Christian unity. See the Web site of the National Council of Churches, http://www.ncccusa.org/unity/worldcommunionsunday.html.

The Bhagavad Gita group at Lake Street Church uses the three-volume commentary by Sri Eknath Easwaran titled *The Bhagavad Gita for Daily Living* (Petaluma, Calif.: Nilgiri, 1979–1984).

For Discussion

1. Would (or does) your church observe World Communion Sunday, an ecumenical Protestant celebration on the first Sunday of October (see above under "For More Information")? Would (or does) your church celebrate an interfaith worship event similar to Lake Street Church's Worldwide Community Sunday? How do you feel about Christians of various denominations sharing the Eucharist or Communion? How do you feel about inviting non-Christians to participate in the Eucharist or Communion?

2. Do you agree with Rev. Thompson that excluding non-Christians from the Eucharist or Communion is "a direct contradiction of what we see in Jesus, who was present with everybody regardless of their standing in society"? What other aspects of Jesus' life and teachings might guide Christians in their relationships with non-Christians? Can you cite biblical passages that stand in tension with Lake Street Church's approach to non-Christians?

3. Peruse the Web sites of the religious groups that participated in the Worldwide Community Sunday service at Lake Street Church (listed in sidebar 6.1). Which groups seem closest to Christianity in beliefs and practices? Which seem furthest removed from Christianity? If you were asked to visit one of these groups in order to learn more about it, which would you feel most comfortable visiting, which least comfortable, and why?

4. The president of the Buddhist Council of the Midwest finds Lake Street Church an appropriate host for the annual international Visakha celebration, especially since the church has "spirituality" (see sidebar 6.2). Peruse the council's Web site (http://www.buddhistcouncilmidwest.org) or other sources on Buddhism for beliefs and practices that seem compatible with Lake Street Church's spirituality.

5. How well do you think Lake Street Church deals with its internal diversity of religious perspectives? Is it possible for conservative or traditional Christians to feel comfortable in a congregation with such an open-ended definition of what it means to be a Christian?

6. Should Lake Street Church drop its affiliation with the American Baptist Churches USA denomination? Should the American Baptist Churches USA drop Lake Street Church from its roster of affiliated congregations? If your congregation comes out of the Baptist heritage, how do you judge Lake Street Church's interpretation of fundamental Baptist principles? Would your denomination, whether Baptist or another, accept Lake Street Church as an affiliated congregation?

7. Revisit the final paragraph of this chapter. Is Lake Street Church a Christian church? Does it represent the future of liberal Protestantism? How important is liberal Protestantism to Christianity as a whole? How important is liberal Protestantism to non-Christian religions?

8. Bible passages: Matthew 9:9–13 and Luke 5:27–32 show Jesus participating in what Rev. Robert Thompson would call radically inclusive table fellowship. The Bhagavad Gita discussion group drew parallels between 1 Corinthians 13 and the Hindu story of the god Krishna filling his flute with divine love and joy.

SEVEN

Bridges to Understanding: St. Lambert Roman Catholic Church

FATHER ANDREW LUCZAK HAD SOME formative experiences growing up in Chicago in the 1940s and 1950s. He remembers his mother befriending all of the families in their ethnically diverse neighborhood along north Ashland Avenue, families with names like Schmidt, Foley, Spagnoli, Bolivar, Pappas, and Mikolajczek. When he had a skin problem, his parents took him to a renowned African American dermatologist who played no favorites with his patients—they all had to wait their turn, no matter what their race or status. As a young man, Fr. Luczak met a Presbyterian minister and his wife who regularly hosted ethnic theme parties in their Hyde Park neighborhood home. Their openness to people of all cultures, races, and religions greatly impressed him.

Father Luczak's college and seminary training introduced him to the diversity within the Catholic Church, with its many clerical orders and liturgical rites. He recalls becoming a "committed ecumenist" during a course titled "Principles of Catholic Ecumenism," taught in 1964 at Loyola University by Fr. David Bowman, S.J., a pioneer in interfaith dialogue. In that course, Fr. Luczak explained, "we were told to visit other churches, temples, and synagogues, to invite interreligious guests to our class, and to attend services. Father Bowman urged us to be mindful of the regulations on *communicatio in sacris,* that is, participation that ends in what amounts to 'practice' or intercommunion." The Second Vatican Council, the historic gathering of Catholic Church leaders in Rome from 1963 to 1965, also had a powerful effect on Fr. Luczak's personal and vocational development, as did the American civil rights movement of that same period. Both taught him the importance of equality, justice, and human dignity in intergroup relations. Vatican II also showed him the church's appreciation of truths and values that can be found in non-Christian religions (see sidebar 7.1).

When Fr. Luczak was appointed St. Lambert's pastor in 1993, the members asked him what he would like for a welcoming

---

SIDEBAR 7.1
Excerpt from "Declaration on the Relation of the Church to Non-Christian Religions" *(Nostra Aetate),* **Second Vatican Council, 1965**

The Catholic Church rejects nothing that is true and holy in these religions. She regards with sincere reverence those ways of conduct and of life, those precepts and teachings which, though differing in many aspects from the ones she holds and sets forth, nonetheless often reflect a ray of that Truth which enlightens all men. Indeed, she proclaims, and ever must proclaim Christ "the way, the truth, and the life" (John 14:6), in whom men may find the fullness of religious life, in whom God has reconciled all things to Himself [cf. 2 Cor. 5:18–19].

The Church, therefore, exhorts her sons, that through dialogue and collaboration with the followers of other religions, carried out with prudence and love and in witness to the Christian faith and life, they recognize, preserve, and promote the good things, spiritual and moral, as well as the sociocultural values found among these men.

Source: http://www.vatican.va.

celebration. He requested a simple potluck dinner to which all the ethnic groups of the parish would contribute their favorite dishes. For Fr. Luczak, this was a perfect symbol of his basic philosophy of celebrating diversity within a context of Catholic spiritual formation. And his new church home was the perfect place to implement that philosophy.

Skokie, the near north suburb where St. Lambert is located, experienced dramatic demographic changes in the years leading up to and during Fr. Luczak's tenure at the church. Ethnically, Skokie's population went from 99 percent white in 1970 to 69 percent white in 2000, and the largest new minority groups were Asians (21 percent) and Hispanics (6 percent). Baha'is, Buddhists, Hindus, and Muslims diversified the religious mix of the area, which already had a large number of Jewish residents. The local clergy association, a particularly active circle of ministers and rabbis established in the 1970s, began to reach out to these new religious groups, for instance, by organizing an annual interfaith Thanksgiving service, which is broadcast on the local public access television channel. They have also discussed opening their membership to clergy and lay leaders from other religions, a move they know will significantly alter the association's self-identity.

The ethnic diversity of St. Lambert's parish reflects that of the town and includes Assyrians, Cubans, Filipinos, Mexicans, Poles, Romanians, Russians, and Sri Lankans. The church's motto, "A Christian Community Welcoming All People," proclaims its inclusiveness. As a parish school board official told us, he chose to live in Skokie because of its diversity, and he loves St. Lambert for its response to that variety. The church "is a place where diversity is not just *tolerated,* it's *celebrated,*" he said proudly. The various ethnic groups are integrated into the overall life of the congregation, and their ethnic Catholic celebrations and practices are regularly featured. A Cuban American couple who joined the church long before Fr. Luczak arrived told us about his role in this:

> Husband: "We basically became more involved in the church after Fr. Luczak. Father Luczak has done wonderful things in terms of getting more people involved."

Interviewer: "How does he do that?"

Wife: "He appeals to the different cultural groups."

Husband: "He appeals to every cultural group and gets everyone involved."

Wife: "He tries to, like, the special needs and the special interests that he notices that the different groups have...he tries to figure out, okay, how can we celebrate that to get that particular group more involved?"

Interviewer: "And that's been nice for them?"

Husband: "Very nice."

One example of St. Lambert's celebration of diversity is its annual speakers series called Dialogues in Sacred Culture, subtitled Exploring the Many Cultures that Express and Enrich Our Faith. As the church's promotional materials describe it, "Dialogues in Sacred Culture is dedicated to an inclusive appreciation of the Catholic heritage...all cultures celebrating as One Family...many colors, one mosaic...many voices praising God in harmony!" (ellipses in original). Topics over the years have included African American, Asian Indian, Filipino, Hispanic, and Slavic expressions of Catholicism. The series also expands the circle of spiritual exploration beyond the diverse Catholic world by welcoming "a positive relationship with believers of other religious traditions, for to be religious in today's pluralistic society is to be interreligious," according to the promotional materials. Speakers have addressed the following topics: Orthodox Christian iconography, Celtic spirituality, Asian ancestor veneration, the Confucian vision of community, contemporary Catholic-Jewish relations, and medieval Catholic-Muslim relations. The series "is dedicated to an inclusive appreciation of the Catholic heritage and a respectful study of other religious traditions...[and also] aims to build greater harmony within the Church and in the larger community."

Pursuant to the spirit of Vatican II, other programs and initiatives at St. Lambert delve deeper into the truths and values found in non-Christian religions. For instance, in recent years St. Lambert took leadership in the formal Buddhist-Catholic dialogue that has occurred in the Chicago area since 1991. Initiated by participants from the Chicago Archdiocese's Office for Ecumenical and Interreligious Affairs, DePaul University (a Vincentian university), the Buddhist Council of the Midwest, and a local Thai Buddhist temple, the group met monthly in the early years to discuss topics such as the human predicament, violence, and social action. Meetings slacked off a bit as participants became involved in the 1993 Parliament of the World's Religions in Chicago, as well as in ongoing activities sponsored by the parliament's organizing body, the Council for a Parliament of the World's Religions (see the introduction to this book). However, major national Buddhist-Catholic encounters kept the idea alive locally, especially for the 1996 Gethsemani Encounter at the Trappist monastery in Kentucky made famous by Thomas Merton, which Fr. Luczak attended. In 2000 he and the president of the Buddhist Council of the Midwest revived the local Buddhist-Catholic dialogue group. Discussion topics have included Buddhist and Catholic iconography, similarities and differences in meditation traditions, and the September 11, 2001, terrorist attacks on the United States.

The centerpiece of St. Lambert's interreligious programming is the "Bridges to Understanding" lecture/discussion series, which lends its name to the title of this chapter. In Fr. Luczak's first year at St. Lambert (1993), the Catholic Theological Union seminary in Chicago chose the parish to host a ministry practicum on world religions. Father Luczak's early newsletter descriptions of the program, then called "Interfaith Dialogue," explained that it stemmed from an "interreligious consciousness" and created a "threshold" for religious interaction at St. Lambert Church. An interreligious consciousness, wrote Fr. Luczak, recognizes the fact of religious diversity and the ways in which it "impacts our Catholic identity and everyday lives."

"Catholics should know their faith and live their tradition," he observed, "but no Catholic today can do *only* that. Our neighbors are Protestant, Jewish, Hindu, Buddhist, and Moslem....To live in harmony is to have understanding that comes from dialogue. Dialogue with other religious traditions is not a defensive apologetic nor an aggressive campaign to 'convert' others. When people meet, it should be with respect. That respect can achieve not only an atmosphere of tolerance but mutual enrichment." Sidebar 7.2 shows an excerpt from Pope John Paul II's encyclical *Redemptoris Missio*, which appeared in a 1994 St. Lambert newsletter article on the Interfaith Dialogue series.

The first year featured field trips to local religious centers such as the Hindu Temple of Greater Chicago, the Muslim Community Center, and Bultasa, a Korean Buddhist temple. The seminarian who led the series reflected on the worship experience at the Hindu temple. "That evening we were witnessing a blessed ritual of one of the most ancient religions in the world," he wrote, "and a window was open to us in our first attempts, as part of the Interfaith Dialogue Group, to understand and respect other faith traditions. We did not come with offerings of flowers or fruits but with an offering of open hearts to receive the answers for our questions. And so we left the temple feeling that in some way we had been introduced into one more of the deep mysteries of God, who is the source and revealer of all Truth."

A 1995 speaker series addressed the topic "Bridges to Understanding," which stuck as the title for the ongoing program. Its simple goal, Fr. Luczak told us, is to discover points of harmony

---

SIDEBAR 7.2
Excerpt from *Redemptoris Missio*, Pope John Paul II, 1990

Other religions constitute a positive challenge for the Church: they stimulate her both to discover and acknowledge the signs of Christ's presence and of the working of the Spirit as well as to examine more deeply her own identity and to bear witness to the fullness of revelation which she has received for the good of all.

Source: St. Lambert newsletter article on the Interfaith Dialogue series (Fall 1994).

and enrichment in encountering other religions. The program logo shows a covered bridge surrounded by the symbols of six religious traditions: a cross for Christianity in the twelve o'clock position, then, moving clockwise, an eight-spoked wheel for Buddhism, a sacred hoop for Native American traditions, a Star of David for Judaism, a yin-yang symbol for Chinese religions, and an Om symbol for Hinduism. The church's promotional materials describe the program as follows: "Bridges link separated shores. Bridges to Understanding are human connections—persons, ideas, shared experiences that open the way to harmony and mutual enlightenment. 'Bridges to Understanding' is an interreligious series that recognizes in the meeting of traditions the most hopeful sign that we can learn from each other, strengthen our own religious identities, respect diversity, and live in peace."

Topics over the years have included "Buddhist Insight Meditation: A Means of Developing Christian Spirituality," "Native American Peoples and the Global Community: Ancient Spiritual Insights Contributing to the Future," "Master Stories of Judaism and Christianity," "Two Sides of Tao: Taoism and Christian Meditation," and "Sadhana [Hindu spiritual practice]: A Way to God." These sessions are led by Catholics or non-Catholics, clergy or nonclergy, as the case may be. A session on the topic "Sufism: Friendship with God," led by the director of the Catholic-Muslim studies program at the Catholic Theological Union seminary, was described thusly in the promotional materials:

> The Muslim journey toward...deep God-consciousness
> through unrelenting self-awareness is the way of the "Sufi."
> This session will attempt to convey only the slightest whiff
> from the Sufi garden of spiritual insights and mysteries by
> discussing some of the more basic features of Sufi teaching
> and by sampling some of the poetic wisdom of great medieval
> Sufi masters.

Father Luczak hopes church members will come to understand that such encounters with other religions can open up and enlarge their own identity as Catholics. He was once asked by a skeptical parishioner, "What can I possibly learn from a Hindu?" "A great deal," he replied and proceeded to explain the Hindu notion of *margs*, or "ways" to salvation, such as the way of knowledge, the way of service, and the way of devotion, all of which are present in the Catholic tradition.

Theologically, Fr. Luczak draws his primary direction from *Nostra Aetate*, but he also applies St. Anselm's famous notion of "faith seeking understanding" to his own interfaith journey—his faith as a Catholic who is seeking an understanding of the faith expressed in other religious contexts. Catholics should bring something of their own faith to such encounters, but they should also watch, learn, and perhaps discover something in their own tradition they may have neglected. He learned this in his first interfaith visit in college. At an Episcopal church, he saw worshipers immersed in high church rituals that he himself was ready to discard at the time. The beauty of the service and his experience of the holy in it taught him an appreciation of another religion, as well as his own.

As to biblical sources for his interfaith approach, Fr. Luczak noted the passage in John's Gospel about many dwelling places in the Father's house. He also talked about Jesus' perspective on the "outsiders" of his day, as seen in parables like that of the Good Samaritan and in his encounters with the Roman centurion and the woman at the well. Father Luczak singled out Peter's vision in the book of Acts as "a marvelous, liberating passage" that reveals Peter's reluctance to be stretched toward welcoming Gentiles into the Kingdom of God.

Over the years, Fr. Luczak's attempts to stretch St. Lambert's multicultural and interreligious horizons were not always accepted or understood. He recalls one program early in his tenure at the church that drew pointed criticism, the Asian Lunar New Year celebration. He took great care in planning the first one in 1994, researching various aspects of Asian history and culture and consulting a Maryknoll missionary and his Chinese art teacher in order to ensure authenticity. He installed a small, temporary shrine for ancestor veneration in the sanctuary for use in a celebration modeled on a Catholic service used in Hong Kong. Sharp criticism came from an anonymous, old-line parishioner in a letter to Fr. Luczak: "May you fall on your face on what you are doing to the church."

Other old-liners threatened to leave the church because of the Lunar New Year celebration and the larger parish programming changes it signified. More moderate reactions prevailed, however. Some parishioners were perplexed, others indifferent, and still others simply preferred more familiar cultural expressions of their faith. Father Luczak expressed his regrets over the situation in an interview with us. He felt that people did not understand what he was trying to accomplish with the Lunar New Year celebration. After trying it a second year, he dropped the idea.

Father Luczak pastored St. Lambert Church for more than a decade before being transferred to another parish in a nearby suburb. He has served in two capacities for the Chicago Archdiocese over the years, as adjunct staff in the area of Buddhist-Catholic relations for the Office of Ecumenical and Interreligious Affairs, and as an advisor on Asian affairs for the Office of Ethnic Ministries. He also serves as a trustee for the Council for a Parliament of the World's Religions. At the time of our research we asked Fr. Luczak whether he thought St. Lambert's multicultural and interreligious programming would continue after his departure. He said his successor would determine that. We suspect that the parish's emphasis on multicultural Catholicism is likely to endure, but that would not necessarily ensure the continuation of an interreligious agenda. Certainly St. Lambert's motto, "A Christian Community Welcoming All People," could endure without building "bridges to understanding" with non-Christian religions.

For More Information

The contact information for St. Lambert Roman Catholic Church is 8148 N. Karlov, Skokie, IL 60076; phone 847-673-5090; http://www.stlambert.org. See the following Web sites for interreligious activities at various levels of the Roman Catholic Church: http://www.archchicago.org/departments/ecumenical/eia.shtm (Office for Ecumenical and Interreligious Affairs, Archdiocese of Chicago); http://www.usccb.org/seia (Secretariat for Ecumenical and Interreligious Affairs, U.S. Conference of Catholic Bishops); and http://www.vatican.va/roman_curia/pontifical_councils/iterelg/

index.htm (Pontifical Council for Interreligious Dialogue, the Vatican). In 2008 the Pontifical Council for Interreligious Dialogue established the Catholic-Muslim Forum in response to an open letter from 138 Muslim scholars to various Christian leaders; see Cindy Wooden, "Vatican, Muslim Representatives Establish Catholic-Muslim Forum," Catholic News Service, http://www.catholicnews.com/data/stories/cns/0801242.htm (March 5, 2008).

Documents of the Second Vatican Council (Vatican II), such as the "Declaration on the Relation of the Church to Non-Christian Religions" *(Nostra Aetate)*, and papal encyclicals, such as John Paul II's 1990 *Redemptoris Missio,* are archived on the Vatican's Web site, http://www.vatican.va.

The 1996 Gethsemani Encounter at Gethsemani Abbey in Kentucky is described in Donald W. Mitchell and James A. Wiseman, eds., *The Gethsemani Encounter: A Dialogue on the Spiritual Life by Buddhist and Christian Monastics* (New York: Continuum, 1997). A Gethsemani II conference, held in April of 2003, brought together forty Buddhist and Catholic monastics to discuss the topic of suffering; for a report on that conference, see the Spring 2003 newsletter of the Society for Buddhist-Christian Studies. The society was founded in 1987 and includes scholars and practitioners from a variety of Buddhist and Christian traditions. Its journal is titled *Buddhist-Christian Studies,* and its Web site is http://www.society-buddhist-christian-studies.org. A fiftieth anniversary edition of Thomas Merton's autobiography, *The Seven Storey Mountain,* came out in 1998 (New York: Harcourt Brace).

For Discussion

1. Local clergy associations like the one mentioned in this chapter often include both Christian pastors and Jewish rabbis. How might opening membership to clergy from other religions alter such an association's self-identity? Would this raise questions for Christian clergy that are substantively different from those in their current participation with rabbis?

2. Do you agree with the statement from the Dialogues in Sacred Culture series at St. Lambert Church that "to be religious in today's pluralistic society is to be interreligious"?

3. Father Andrew Luczak wrote, "Dialogue with other religious traditions is not a defensive apologetic nor an aggressive campaign to 'convert' others." Compare his view with that of others in this book. In your opinion, should apologetics (the rational defense of the Christian faith) and seeking to convert non-Christians play some role in Christian participation in interfaith dialogue?

4. Responding to a parishioner's question, "What can I possibly learn from a Hindu?" Fr. Luczak replied, "A great deal." What can Catholics (or Christians in general) learn from other religions? What can other religions learn from Catholics (or Christians in general)?

5. Consider the wording of the two sidebar excerpts in this chapter, from Vatican II's "Declaration on the Relation of the Church to Non-Christian Religions" (*Nostra Aetate*) and Pope John Paul II's encyclical *Redemptoris Missio*. Summarize the view of the relationship between the truth claims of Christianity and other religions expressed in these authoritative Catholic statements.

6. What was it about the Asian Lunar New Year celebration that offended some members of St. Lambert Church? Father Luczak told us that the Chinese, Korean, and Vietnamese members felt very much at home with the celebration, while other members, both whites and immigrants from areas in Asia less influenced by the Chinese culture, exhibited a range of responses from interest to indifference. What does this say about the role of culture in religious practices?

7. Discuss the relationship between the sentiments expressed in St. Lambert's motto, "A Christian Community Welcoming All People," and its interfaith series, "Bridges to Understanding." Are the two notions inherently linked, or were they linked at St. Lambert only through Fr. Luczak's initiative?

8. Bible passages: Father Luczak draws upon John 14:2 (many dwelling places in the Father's house), Luke 10:25–37 (the parable of the Good Samaritan), Matthew 8:5–13 (Jesus and the Roman centurion), John 4:1–30 (Jesus and the woman at the well), and Acts 10 (in Fr. Luczak's words, "a marvelous, liberating passage" about Peter's reluctance to welcome Gentiles into the Kingdom of God).

EIGHT

Unity in Spirituality: The Focolare Movement

CHICAGO'S ANNUAL BUD BILLIKEN PARADE is the largest African American parade in the country, a back-to-school promotion that emphasizes black pride, hope, and success. The parade features floats from a variety of African American groups and businesses. One float is sponsored by the American Society of Muslims (ASM), the largest African American Muslim group in the United States, followers of mainstream Sunni Islam under the leadership of the late Imam Warith Deen Mohammed. In 2003 the ASM invited the Catholic spirituality movement called Focolare to cosponsor their float in the Bud Billiken Parade. The question surely crossed the minds of parade-goers that day as the float passed by carrying African American Muslims and white Catholics in a show of interfaith harmony: "Who are these Focolare?"

The Focolare movement began in 1943 with a remarkable woman, the late Chiara Lubich. In the midst of the despair of World War II Italy, Ms. Lubich brought together a small group of young Catholic friends who rediscovered the powerful communal love and spirituality of the early Christians. Focolare is Italian for "hearth or fireside," evoking the feeling of an intimate family warmed by God's spirit. The movement took to heart Jesus' prayer in John 17 that his followers might be one.

As Chiara Lubich wrote, "Initially we believed that we were simply living the Gospel, but meanwhile the Holy Spirit was at work emphasising some words of the Gospel which were to become a new spiritual current—the spirituality of unity." This gave rise to a communitarian renewal movement expressed most notably in the living arrangements of its core members, including several Focolare "minicities" around the world, each called a permanent Mariapolis (after Mary, Mother of Unity), such as the ones in Loppiano, Italy (the first, established in 1964) and Sao Paolo, Brazil, as well as Mariapolis Luminosa in Hyde Park, New York. Smaller Focolare communal groups also exist, like the one in Chicago, which has a women's residence on the city's South Side and a men's residence in suburban Oak Park. These do not function as local congregations within the Catholic institutional structure—the Focolare attend their own parishes. Most Focolare do not reside communally but live out their spirituality in family and work settings. The movement, which claims more than two million lay and clergy adherents in 182 countries, received papal approval from Pope John XXIII in 1962 and had the strong support of Pope John Paul II (see sidebar 8.1).

The Focolare movement's interfaith activities originated in London in 1977, when Chiara Lubich received the prestigious Templeton Prize for Progress in Religion. As she reported the story, she felt a special presence of God among the audience, which included representatives of several world religions. She knew then that the Focolare must begin what she called "dialogues of love" with spiritually minded members of other faiths. In 1979 Ms. Lubich met with Nikkyo Niwano, founder of the Japanese Buddhist lay movement called Rissho Kosei-kai and a leader in the World Conference of Religions for Peace, a major global inter-faith organization. This led to a close working relationship with both groups on peace and humanitarian issues. Over the years, the Focolare have entered into dialogues with Buddhists, Hindus, Jews, Muslims, Shintoists, Sikhs, and Zoroastrians. As the Focolare Web site describes the relationships, "There are about 30,000 members of other religions who live in their own measure the spirit of the Movement and are committed to the same aims." The Focolare have participated in several major interfaith gatherings, includ-ing the Interreligious Assembly at the Vatican in 1999, the Faith

---

SIDEBAR 8.1

Excerpt from "Letter of the Holy Father [Pope John Paul II] to Chiara Lubich, Foundress and President of the Focolare Movement," on the Occasion of Her Eightieth Birthday in 2000

In the footsteps of Jesus crucified and abandoned, you began the Focolare Movement to help the men and women of our time experience God's tenderness and fidelity, by living the grace of fraternal communion among them, in order to be joyful and credible heralds of the Gospel.

As I entrust you and all the good you have done in these long years to the protection of Mary, Mother of Unity, I invoke upon you the power and light of the Holy Spirit so that you will continue to be a courageous witness of faith and charity not only among the members of the Focolare Movement but also among those you meet on your path.

Source: http://www.vatican.va/holy_father/john_paul_ii/letters/2000/documents/hf_jp-ii_let_20000122_chiaralubich_en.html.

Communities Together conference in Washington, D.C., in 2000, and World Youth Day in Toronto in 2002.

The touchstone biblical imperative for the Focolare's interfaith activities is the Golden Rule, which they find in virtually all religions: Do unto others as you would have them do unto you (Matthew 7:12). A speaker at the Mariapolis conference we attended (described in this chapter) explained:

> The basis of all this is love. That really finds an echo in every religion and in every culture.... So, that sentence [the Golden Rule] became a basis for our relationship with one another. We realized that God wants us all to be perfect in love, and so we have this way of trying to love that we call the art of loving. And this is also the basis for our meetings together, the art

of loving, which means that we want to love everyone, be the first to love, be concrete in our love with others, do something practical, and then make yourself one with the other person in order to reach this bond of unity. In our meetings with one another, with people of other religions, we share how we are trying to live this art of loving.

The Focolare use the "technique" of making themselves "one with the others." As their Web site explains, "it is a practice which demands the complete emptying of oneself in order to become one with the others, 'placing oneself in the others' shoes,' penetrating the very meaning it has for the other to be Hindu, Muslim, Jewish, etc." This does not entail compromising Christian beliefs but rather being open to "an encounter of the soul, of people who have made a choice of God, who want to share this life of union with God," says Marco DeSalvo, codirector of the Chicago Focolare community. "We don't have any other goal or program to convert or proselytize," he explained to us. "Our goal is to live for God, to be Christians. Because they [dialogue partners from other religions] are open, very wonderful, spiritual people, they are sensitive to the divine."

Paola Santostefano, the other codirector of the Chicago Focolare community, continued: "If you love everyone, to love always, to see Jesus in everybody, to love your enemy—then the love becomes mutual, then this is the basis to reach out to people....For us it is encountering Jesus in every person." This is the "art of loving," in Paola's words. "We love everybody who comes our way."

The American Society of Muslims (ASM), mentioned at the outset of this chapter, came the Focolare's way in the mid-1990s. By then Imam Warith Deen Mohammed had moved the ASM out of the quasi-Islamic identity of the original Nation of Islam, founded by his father, the Honorable Elijah Muhammad, and into mainstream Sunni Islam. Imam Mohammed changed the name of the group—the old Nation of Islam name and identity continue under Minister Louis Farrakhan (see chapter 9)—and changed the spelling of his own last name to mark this significant transition. Known for his personal piety, Imam Mohammed stressed the spiritual aspects of Islam in the group's new direction.

In 1995 William Cardinal Keeler of the Secretariat for Ecumenical and Interreligious Affairs of the United States Conference of Catholic Bishops asked the Focolare to establish a relationship with the ASM as a means of enhancing Catholic-Muslim dialogue. The Chicago Focolare community invited Imam Mohammed to visit its house on the city's South Side. As one Focolare leader recounts, when Imam Mohammed heard about Chiara Lubich's experiences and vision, he leaned forward in his chair and said, "I want my people to know about this. I am coming back." His hosts presented him with a book about Lubich, to which he replied, "I am going to read this before I go to bed tonight." Thus began the interfaith and interracial relationship between the African American ASM and the Focolare movement, whose membership, although international, includes relatively few African Americans.

On an occasion both groups consider historic, in May of 1997 the ASM invited Chiara Lubich to speak at the Malcolm Shabazz Mosque in Harlem, the mosque named after the well-known Nation of Islam leader, Malcolm X, who changed his name to El Hajj Malik el-Shabazz late in life (see sidebar 8.2). "We invited her because she is a very special woman," Imam Mohammed told the Focolare magazine, *Living City.* "And what I have seen is that you [Focolare] represent a message of the Gospel that all people can benefit from. It's the message of love, the message of peace, the message of sharing and caring about each other. You do it so well that you've convinced me that it's genuine."

The Focolare and the American Society of Muslims have gathered together in many venues across the United States and abroad. The ASM's periodical, *Muslim Journal,* regularly covers these events. For instance, it ran several articles leading up to the November 2000 Faith Communities Together conference in Washington, D.C., including an interview of Imam Mohammed conducted by Chicago Focolare codirector Paola Santostefano. In its December 1, 2000, issue, *Muslim Journal* reprinted the entire text of Chiara Lubich's speech at the conference and stated that it captured "the true meaning of 'receiving G-d's Inspiration.'" ("G-d" is a convention used out of respect for the divine name.)

SIDEBAR 8.2

Excerpt from Chiara Lubich's Speech at Malcolm Shabazz Mosque, Harlem, New York City, May 18, 1997

From our very first contacts with Muslims, we have been deeply struck by the affinity that exists between our two religions that trace their roots back to Abraham: belief in one God who is compassionate and merciful, total dedication to God's will, and a high esteem for Jesus and for Mary, his Mother.

But what immediately made us feel especially close to our Muslim brothers and sisters was the fact that we share with you a profound faith in the love of God.

Source: *Living City: The Magazine for a United World* (July 1997).

The two groups have also shared some memorable experiences in Rome. In 2003 the relationship between the Focolare and the ASM was featured at a conference titled "Call to a New Vision of Others and of Ourselves through Interreligious Dialogue: Focus on Islam," sponsored by the Service of Documentation and Study, a consortium of Catholic missionary societies. Presenters Jo-Ellen Karstens of the Focolare and Imam David Shaheed of the ASM described the locally based program called Encounters in the Spirit of Universal Brotherhood, which grew out of the Washington, D.C., conference, wherein mixed groups of Focolare and ASM members meet for dialogue every three to four months in cities across the United States. According to reports, the Rome conference attendees were astounded that Catholics and Muslims could be so amiable with each other. During a private audience with Pope John Paul II during this conference, the Holy Father told the presenters, "I wish you every success."

Says an ASM member about one of the continuing gatherings of the two groups, held every two to three years in Rome, it was "an experience only God could have directed." "It was like a Hajj [the Muslim pilgrimage to Mecca]. But it was better yet because we were in the company of our newly found sisters and brothers of the Focolare."

To get a firsthand feeling for the Focolare way, as well as the relationship between the movement and the American Society of Muslims, we attended part of the five-day Mariapolis 2003 conference held in Valparaiso, Indiana. Such gatherings offer temporary immersion into the communitarian spirituality of a permanent Mariapolis. The theme for Mariapolis 2003 was "Unity in Diversity: All One Family." Facing the opening-day crowd of three hundred people, the MC declared the goal of the conference: "Toward a harmonious living in the human family." "This is an experiment of going out to people who are different, in love," he continued. "We build this city with those who are different, but in unity. This is an experience of being one world."

The first panel of the conference included several veteran Mariapolis participants who shared their testimonies about how the Focolare movement has blessed their lives. One married couple, both of whom had been raised in Focolare families, recounted their first test together of putting faith in God when the husband's employer offered him an opportunity to relocate. Through the experience, they learned to focus on living in the present moment. The wife gained peace of mind from an e-mail from the Focolare movement emphasizing the importance of believing in God's love. One day their young son surprised them by saying, "I need to go to Mariapolis. I need to learn how to love better."

Linda, an African American Muslim woman from Detroit, spoke about the first time a Focolare group visited her mosque. She immediately felt their love and was impressed at how they placed God first in their lives. Her five-year-old grandson called the Focolare "the nicest people in the whole world." "You have all of my love and unity," Linda told the conference audience. "I thank God for having the foresight to bring us together as an example to the whole world."

A panel on "Our Experience of Universal Brotherhood with the American Society of Muslims" included presenters from both the Focolare movement and the ASM, who shared their mutual perspectives and experiences. Following are a few vignettes from the presentations.

In 1999 the first annual "Friends of Clara Mohammed School Award" was presented to Chiara Lubich by the Clara Mohammed School in Milwaukee, Wisconsin. Named after the wife of the Honorable Elijah Muhammad and the mother of Imam Warith Deen Mohammed, Clara Mohammed Schools are the parochial education arm of the American Society of Muslims. The award seemed especially appropriate to the ASM since "Chiara" is the Italian equivalent of the English "Clara." One imam and his wife have even named their daughter Chiara in honor of the Focolare movement's founder.

An imam in Kansas City reserves a room in his home for visiting Focolare members. One Focolare panelist recounted his recent visit:

> I was there just in April, and I have to say that I was so edified.... They have seven children in the house. They all clear out one room for me to stay in, so I am part of the family. It is beautiful, the atmosphere of prayer in that home, because when it is time to pray, the dining room is cleared aside so that it can be a prayer room, the little girls put on their veils, they say their prayers. The most beautiful thing is that before dawn you hear the prayer call, and you hear the little feet going down the stairs because even the four-year-old—she doesn't want to miss out on anything—goes down to pray before dawn every morning. And Sunday morning, I was there, and I came down the stairs, it goes right into the living room, and there were the three teenagers sitting there studying the Qur'an, and this was at 6 o'clock in the morning on a Sunday morning. Their mother said, "I am so sorry that they disturbed you." And I said, "No, no, don't worry." She said, "They do that every Sunday. They spend an hour praying and studying the Qur'an." So, it made me think, I will have to improve my prayer life. This family is imbued with prayer. There is so much that we have learned from one another and shared with one another.

Imam David Shaheed spoke of his experiences in Rome. He was the ASM copresenter at the 2003 SEDOS conference of Catholic missionary societies, and he also attended the 1999 Interreligious Assembly at the Vatican. He keeps a photograph from Rome in his chambers as an Indiana state judge. "There is not a day that I go into my office that I don't think of all of you and Chiara," he told the Mariapolis audience. In an interview for *Living City* magazine, Imam Shaheed elaborated on how his Rome experiences have changed his perspective as a judge: "Now, in the court room where I work, each person that comes in front of me is no longer a number. He or she is a person...and if I can show to each one that same love that I have received, then there is hope that their lives can change, too."

An imam from Chicago expressed his gratitude for the relationship between the American Society of Muslims and the Focolare movement: "This has been a powerful union, and it has been a wonderful model for the world....The world is looking for models, and to show that so many things can be bridged, so many things can be overcome, so many things can be put aside is an example for the world. And we thank God for this." Like the Indiana judge, this imam has also benefited from his interaction with the Focolare in his vocation as an emergency room physician. He has a new awareness that

> it is not just a physician-patient relationship, it is a physician-God-patient relationship—that God is highlighted in that relationship....To love moment by moment and to make God the first one in your life is what we do as Muslims. To be the first to make a move and to respond first with your heart and not just with your mind and to go out of your way....So this relationship has rekindled that in my heart. And on a very personal level, I feel that it made me a better doctor, that now it is no longer a job, it is indeed a service again. It is a service, and it is a worshipful service.

Mariapolis 2003 featured a daily Catholic Mass just before lunch. A Focolare acquaintance explained to our researcher that the communion was closed to non-Catholics. "It is suffering that the table still cannot be shared," she apologized. Paola Santostefano and Marco DeSalvo, the codirectors of the Chicago

Focolare community, placed this issue in context in the following written statement to us:

> At the Mariapolis a special room is prepared for the Muslims so that they can perform their daily prayer in an environment suited to the requirements of their religion. Some Focolare members join them, but in accordance with the directives from the Pontifical Council for Interreligious Dialogue, they stand respectfully in the back of the room as the Muslims recite their prayer. In the same way the daily Catholic Eucharist is open to everyone, although communion is offered only to those who are in union with the Catholic Church. This distinction between the various religious traditions is greatly appreciated by all those who participate, since it allows each believer to worship according to their own belief, and gives witness to the unity in diversity among us.

Although the word "dialogue" is often used in describing the relationship between the Focolare movement and non-Christian religions, those most intimately involved find that word inadequate. "The relationship with the Focolare cannot be called a 'dialogue,'" explains an ASM imam from Milwaukee. "It's much deeper than that, much more profound. We really love one another. We are a family."

In other contexts, interfaith dialogue may stem from the desire to address theological differences. "We don't start from the theological differences between the world religions," says Marco DeSalvo of the Chicago Focolare community, who prefers the phrase "dialogue of life." He points to the importance of Jesus' prayer for unity in John 17:

> We look at the whole Gospel through this sentence, the command of Jesus "that we all may be one." This was the quote that struck Chiara [Lubich] from the beginning within the Gospel. She and her first companions felt drawn to that; that was their call in life, like they were made to work for that, to respond to this testament of Jesus Christ. I feel our dialogue with the Muslims or any dialogue that we have comes

from that, which doesn't mean that all may be Christians or Catholics but that we all may be one—one humanity.

"You are writing about diversity," Paola Santostefano of the Chicago Focolare community kidded us, "but we don't focus on diversity.... The emphasis for us is [that] every person we meet is one to be loved. We don't look at the diversity."

That is what Chiara Lubich meant by a "dialogue of love."

For More Information

The Focolare movement's international Web site is http://www.focolare.org. The Web site for the movement's periodical, *Living City: The Magazine for a United World*, is http://www.livingcitymagazine.com. Chiara Lubich's speech at Malcolm Shabazz Mosque, Harlem, New York City, May 18, 1997 (excerpted in sidebar 8.2), was printed in the July 1997 edition of *Living City*. The Chicago Focolare community can be reached at P.O. Box 53426, Chicago, IL 60653.

The Vatican's Web site is http://www.vatican.va. Information about the Focolare movement from the Vatican's perspective can be retrieved by using the search function. The "Letter of the Holy Father [Pope John Paul II] to Chiara Lubich, Foundress and President of the Focolare Movement" (excerpted in sidebar 8.1), can be found at http://www.vatican.va/holy_father/john_paul_ii/letters/2000/documents/hf_jp-ii_let_20000122_chiara-lubich_en.html.

The American Society of Muslims (ASM) has undergone several name changes since 1975 and has been in transition since Imam Warith Deen Mohammed's retirement in 2003. The Web site for ASM's periodical, *Muslim Journal*, is http://muslimjournal.net. Two scholarly overviews of African American Islamic history and groups are Aminah Beverly McCloud, *African American Islam* (New York: Routledge, 1995), and Richard Brent Turner, *Islam in the African-American Experience* (Bloomington: Indiana University Press, 1997).

The Web site of the World Conference of Religions for Peace is http://www.wcrp.org. Chiara Lubich was an honorary president of the organization, and Imam Warith Deen Mohammed once sat on its governing board.

For Discussion

1. Discuss the Focolare movement's type of spirituality, particularly its notion of communitarian spirituality. What advantages and disadvantages might the communal-living arrangements of Focolare's core members have for an individual's spiritual expression? How effective do you think temporary immersion into the communitarian spirituality of a permanent Mariapolis, like the one mentioned in this chapter, can be?

2. What do you think of the Focolare's basic assumption that spirituality can unite people within the Catholic Church, across Christian denominations, and even across religions? Is an encounter of the soul between people who have chosen God, to cite one Focolare leader, enough to overcome historical divisions between religious groups? Is there anything else that might bring unity across such boundaries?

3. The Focolare do not compromise their Catholic beliefs and practices in interacting with other religions. Discuss the implications of this stance. Could an uncompromising position in certain contexts, like the closed communion at a Mariapolis gathering, jeopardize interfaith relations?

4. One Focolare leader speaks of "encountering Jesus in every person." How might non-Christians respond to this sentiment? Speculate on the language non-Christians could use in interfaith encounters, perhaps "encountering Buddha in every person." How do you respond to such sentiments as a Christian?

5. Discuss the interfaith and interracial relationship between the American Society of Muslims and the Focolare movement. Does

it surprise you like it did the attendees of the Rome conference of Catholic missionary societies? Which of the testimonies from both sides of this relationship impressed you? Does this relationship provide a model for larger Christian-Muslim interaction?

6. Discuss various kinds of dialogue that can occur between members of different religions. How important is doctrinal dialogue, that is, discussion—and perhaps debate—of beliefs? How would you define a "dialogue of life"? A "dialogue of love"?

7. Bible passages: Two guiding passages for the Focolare movement are John 17 (Jesus' prayer for unity among his followers) and Matthew 7:12 (the Golden Rule).

NINE

Solidarity in the African American Experience: Churches and the Nation of Islam

ON OCTOBER 16, 1995, THE historic Million Man March drew African American men to the nation's capital "in the spirit of atonement to themselves, their families, their communities and their people, seeking forgiveness and reconciliation, and offering their lives in acceptance of their responsibility to uplift and advance themselves and their people." This description of the motivation for the Million Man March comes from the *Final Call,* the official news publication of the Nation of Islam, which reflected on the march's eighth anniversary in 2003.

The idea of the Million Man March originated with Minister Louis Farrakhan, leader of the Nation of Islam, but, as Minister Farrakhan himself points out, Christian participation was vital and significant. More than one-third of the eighty-two dignitaries at the march were Christian leaders, including Rev. Jesse Jackson, Rev. Al Sharpton, Rev. Joseph Lowery, Fr. George Clements, and Rev. Jeremiah Wright. A sample survey of attendees found Baptists to be the largest religious group (38 percent), whereas fewer than 10 percent were Muslims. In Chicago and other cities across the country, African American pastors and church leaders worked hand in hand with the Nation of Islam in organizing support for the event.

Why? Why did these Christians join forces with the Nation of Islam, a group that has drawn African American converts away from churches since its founding under the Honorable Elijah Muhammad in Chicago in the 1930s? Given the controversial nature of the Nation of Islam and Minister Farrakhan, who preaches racial separatism and radical politics and whose version of Islam is considered unorthodox by mainstream Muslims, why would Christian pastors want to associate with this group? (See chapter 8 for a discussion of a mainstream African American Islamic group.) Why, given their differences in religious truth claims, did African American Christians and Muslims unite for the Million Man March?

For answers to these and other questions, we interviewed Rev. Dr. Hycel B. Taylor II, who considers Minister Farrakhan a personal friend as well as a clergy peer. In November of 2003, Dr. Taylor had just returned from a Washington gathering of African American leaders, including Minister Farrakhan, a meeting that sought to rekindle the spirit of the Million Man March and to consider further action.

Emphasizing internal religious differences *disempowers* the African American community, which has been oppressed since slave times, explained Dr. Taylor. Cooperative ventures like the Million Man March

> have not so much to do with our religious differences. In fact,
> it had more to do with what I'm arguing in my own book:
> How do we transcend those differences so we can become a
> formidable force?...We are unwittingly divisive along the lines
> of "You're a black Muslim" or "You're a black Baptist" or "You're
> a black Christian" or "You're a black Hebrew" or whatever.

At the deepest level of communal experience, Dr. Taylor argued, African Americans share "a common fight" and "a common sense of suffering," in the face of which religious distinctions tend to "melt away."

In addition, Dr. Taylor's book, *The African-American Revolt of the Spirit,* presents a theology of the African American experience that he has developed over many years of pastoring, seminary teaching, and social activism. In 1969 Dr. Taylor came to Garrett Evangelical Theological Seminary in Evanston, Illinois, following his seminary education at Vanderbilt University. He established the "Church and the Black Experience" program at Garrett, which he directed until his departure in 1985. In 1972 Dr. Taylor was appointed senior pastor of Evanston's Second Baptist Church, a congregation that he molded during his thirty-year tenure into what the sociologist Shayne Lee describes as "one of the most politically and socially active African American Baptist churches in the Midwest." Paul Tillich and other theologians he studied in seminary, Dr. Taylor points out, taught him that theology derives from human existence, not from doctrines. As he told us, his relationship with the Nation of Islam grew out of "the common reality that we are all black and that we all have the same problems in this racist society." In 1985, a feeling of solidarity in the African American experience impelled Dr. Taylor, when he was president of Operation PUSH, Rev. Jesse Jackson's social action organization, to support Minister Louis Farrakhan in the face of widespread criticism of Farrakhan's views of Judaism. He used that controversy as a teachable moment for his congregation, especially for members who were uninformed about Islam, and has maintained his support for Minister Farrakhan ever since (see sidebar 9.1).

Elaborating on his point about the experiential foundation of an African American theology, Dr. Taylor said he rejects the notion that Christian-Muslim solidarity in the African American community can be understood as a response to growing religious diversity. Framed in this way, "diversity" is a scholarly issue but, even more precisely, a white issue, he argued. The dominant social group in a society considers diversity important, especially those who wish to include minorities in some paternalistic project or another. How shall *we* respond to the religious diversity around *us*?—that is a question framed by the majority. It presupposes that the majority has the option—actually, the power—to include or exclude other groups at their whim, an option unavailable to minorities. For African Americans of all religious identities, the issue is far more practical in that it has to do with survival and solutions: What challenges confront our community, and how can the religions of our community respond effectively? African American Christians

SIDEBAR 9.1
Minister Louis Farrakhan on Dr. Hycel B. Taylor
II and the Million Man March, from a Speech
at Operation PUSH, Chicago, October 14, 1995
(Two Days before the Million Man March)

There are times in history where God intervenes in the affairs of men and chooses among his servants those to whom he speaks in a very special way. Two years ago, the Reverend Dr. Hycel B. Taylor II shared his pulpit with me at his church in Evanston and then came and spoke at Mosque Maryam. And at that time the Reverend Dr. Hycel B. Taylor II spoke of a day when there would be concentration on Almighty God. I sat there and listened to Dr. Hycel B. Taylor II, and I am sure that his words washed my brain and my soul. I never knew that two years after I heard him speak that I would be involved in a day such as he spoke.

Source: Hycel B. Taylor II, *The African-American Revolt of the Spirit* (Chicago: Faith and Freedom, 1996), 219.

who convert to Islam, Dr. Taylor suggested, have not engaged in an academic, comparative analysis of the truth claims of each religion but rather seek the individual and social transformation they find lacking in Christianity.

When we interviewed Dr. Taylor, he was the senior pastor of Pilgrim Baptist Church in Chicago's Bronzeville area, whose history includes famed music director Thomas A. Dorsey, considered by many to be the father of American gospel music. A representative of the Nation of Islam participated in Dr. Taylor's installation in 2002, as did a Jewish rabbi. Nation members attended Pilgrim Baptist, and Dr. Taylor participated in programs at the Nation of Islam's main center, Mosque Maryam, on Chicago's South Side, as he had for years. In addition, Dr. Taylor's daughter, Rev. Chandra

Taylor-Smith, assisted him in pastoring Pilgrim Baptist Church. A Harvard Divinity School graduate, Rev. Taylor-Smith agreed with her father's assessment of the role played by the African American experience in Christian-Muslim relationships. "That shared experience is so important—all of us experience racism in this country," she told us. She also pointed out that a significant line of scholarship maintains, like her father, that most African American converts to the Nation of Islam have joined "because they felt like Christians couldn't help them address some of these issues [of racism]."

Especially in her studies at Harvard, Rev. Taylor-Smith has been exposed to many of the world's religions. She has never felt the need to convert to any of them herself, however, nor has she felt called to convert others to Christianity. At a Chicago area, denominationally based college where she once taught, the faculty engaged in an intense examination of "what it means to be evangelical and go out and try to transform people." "That has not been my cross to bear," she explained to us. A guiding biblical text for her and her siblings, taught them by their father, has been Psalm 24:1: "The earth is the Lord's and the fullness thereof." "That means everything is God's. That doesn't mean it's just Christian. He also taught us that, as Christians, wherever you go, don't worry about trying to change anybody. They'll do that if they see the light that shines in you but also the light that is in them."

The Reverend Taylor-Smith described a memorable encounter she once had with a student from India who attends the Illinois Institute of Technology, located near Pilgrim Baptist Church. The woman approached her in the neighborhood grocery store and mentioned Rev. Taylor-Smith's sermon the previous Sunday during Pilgrim's celebration of women's month. "What you said meant so much to me," the woman offered, although Rev. Taylor-Smith had not even been aware of her presence at the service. "I said, 'Are you a Christian?' She said, 'No, but I believe that God touches us all.' She espoused a very embracing, ecumenical, transcending kind of theology, if you will. So I invited her back for the Christmas service. And she came, and she testified... about the spirit and love of God, and everybody coming together."

The Reverend Taylor-Smith was pleased that this non-Christian woman felt welcome at Pilgrim Baptist Church, which she was continuing to attend at the time of our interview. In this encounter also, shared experience meant more than dissimilar religious identities, in this case the experience of being touched by what both women considered a divine spirit. Moreover, Rev. Taylor-Smith was more than a little taken by the fact that the Indian woman's given name was the same as her own, Chandra. When her father heard of their encounter in the grocery store, he suggested that the Indian woman might have been an angel.

The Reverend James L. Demus III has been senior pastor of Park Manor Christian Church, a Disciples of Christ congregation located a few blocks from the Nation of Islam's Mosque Maryam, since 1985. Members of both congregations live together in the neighborhood and share their daily lives and their deep concerns for the African American community. Shared experience, Rev. Demus also agrees, not abstract notions of comparative religion or interfaith dialogue, sets the African American religious agenda. That experience, he told us, is what brings his members to him, asking the church to address the issues affecting—or afflicting— their community.

That is how he and Park Manor Church got involved with the Million Man March in 1995, as Rev. Demus explained on a PBS news program just days before the march. The partnership began at "the inquiry and the insistence" of a church member who asked, "Rev. Demus, are we going to do anything with this Million Man March?" The question was not framed as "Rev. Demus, what is Islam, and how should Christians respond to it?" Rather, this church member was responding to the Nation of Islam's call for a national gathering to spotlight issues surrounding African American men. As Rev. Demus recounted, the man simply explained, "This march is being called, and I basically think that I need to go."

Shortly after this conversation with the church member, Rev. Demus received a letter that invited him to Minister Louis Farrakhan's home in Chicago to discuss organizing local participation in the Million Man March. Along with sixteen other African American pastors, Rev. Demus met that evening with Minister

Farrakhan and enjoyed a fine, health-conscious Nation of Islam meal and violin music performed by their talented host. When the discussion turned to the matter at hand, Rev. Demus, new to the group, looked around and asked where the rest of the pastors were. How could a mere sixteen pastors accomplish the task, especially with the march now only ten weeks away?

The others replied that, although the planning had been going on for the past year and invitations had been sent to many pastors, only these few who were present had shown interest. At this, Rev. Demus was frank: "With all due respect, Minister Farrakhan, I think I know why they aren't coming." He then proceeded to explain why meeting at Minister Farrakhan's home instead of at one of the churches might not appeal to many pastors and why the prominent display of Minister Farrakhan's picture on publicity materials for the march might have given the impression that this was a personal project that lacked community-wide support.

As a result of this exchange, the group decided to hold the next meeting at Rev. Demus's church. This time two hundred pastors and other Christian leaders showed up. The two hundred swelled to seven hundred the following meeting, and effective organizing for the march commenced. Park Manor Christian Church was selected as the hub of the effort. When church members began to notice all of the activity and the large Nation of Islam presence at their church, they questioned Rev. Demus. Some were unsure of what the Nation of Islam represented. Like Dr. Hycel Taylor with his church, Rev. Demus took the opportunity as a teachable moment and offered study groups on Islam, focusing especially on the Abrahamic roots it shares with Christianity and Judaism. Again this inquiry arose out of practical circumstances rather than theoretical inquisitiveness.

A major organizational task for pastors in Chicago and around the country was to provide buses for participants of the Million Man March. One estimate had as many as two hundred buses coming from Chicago. One included more than thirty homeless men from Matthew House, a Christian-based shelter on Chicago's South Side directed by Rev. Sanja Stinson, a woman minister whose husband, a deacon at their church, was also on the bus. Matthew

House serves both Christian and Muslim clients, who took the initiative to participate in the march. "Basically, the men organized it themselves," Rev. Stinson said. "They saw it, they wanted to get involved, they needed the support, they needed the guidance. We supported it."

The Reverend Stinson downplayed the significance of doctrinal differences between the Nation of Islam and her own Christian faith in this joint effort. "We were saying, 'We're not joining the Nation of Islam; there's some belief factors that we don't believe in.' But the mission of this particular venture was something that we all could collaborate together and agree together on." She calls this "an ecumenical approach," one that sets aside religious distinctions in order to accomplish common social goals. In her mind, the events of September 11, 2001, marked another instance of the necessity for such collaboration: "9/11 was a time where everyone needed to come together, regardless of religious background." For Christians, Rev. Stinson believes, 9/11 called to mind the importance of loving one's enemies and showing forgiveness to one's attackers. Since 9/11, she has seen growing evidence of the "ecumenical approach" among the various religious groups represented in the African American community: "I think that we're leading in that direction. I really see more religions coming together than any [other] time to work out issues with the neighborhood and the community. I've seen them put their religions on the back burner and say, 'Let's come to the table.'"

The year following the Million Man March, Rev. James Demus published his views on what he calls the "encounter" of African American Christians and Muslims in the *Christian Ministry* magazine. In addition to the Million Man March, he wrote, "The Christian and Muslim faithful of our congregations have joined efforts over a number of projects in our community," including voting, prisons, drugs, mentoring, and businesses. "How do I deal with the theological differences between Christianity and the Nation of Islam? Our differences rarely come up unless we are asked to be on opposing sides for a television show." Within the African American community, Islam is not in opposition to Christianity. In fact, there is a more dangerous opposition to both Muslims and Christians, Rev. Demus explained:

> Within the African-American community, the issue is not the Nation of Islam versus Christianity but religion versus the lure of the streets.... We will continue to cooperate with our Muslim neighbors on projects that are mutually beneficial to our communities and to encourage one another in acts of goodwill and faith.... Our common concern has led our congregations to put aside differences in faith and to work together.

As this chapter intimates at times, not everyone in the African American Christian community believes that differences in religious truth claims between Christianity and Islam should be put aside or on the back burner in order to take up common social causes. The concern that some church members expressed about their pastors' involvement with the Nation of Islam included questions about the fundamental compatibility of Christian and Muslim belief systems. Closer to home, Rev. James Demus spoke of tensions in his own family when one member became a Black Hebrew Israelite and in the process rejected his given name, which came from the New Testament. According to Dr. Hycel Taylor, a few Christian groups in the African American community, like the Jehovah's Witnesses, seek to convert Muslims. Moreover, he sees the rise of a new religious conservatism among younger African Americans, perhaps influenced by the larger white Christian conservative movement, which espouses what Dr. Taylor calls a "Jesiology," in which there is only one way to salvation.

Even so, the powerful shared experience of minority status in American society has created a significant measure of solidarity among African American groups that is difficult for the majority members of society to understand. Other labels, even religious ones, seem far less important than that imposed by racism. A theology of the African American experience, according to the Christian pastors in this chapter, offers liberation for all in God's diverse creation (see sidebar 9.2).

SIDEBAR 9.2
Principle 1 of the "Ten Principles of Spiritual Empowerment for African-American Social/ Political Movement," by Hycel B. Taylor II

You shall let nothing separate you from God, yourself as an individual, or your African-American brothers and sisters as a racially designated and homogeneous social group among other racially designated and homogenous social groups within the human family. This is your loving and sacred obligation. To do this does not suggest racial superiority or reverse racism. Let no one impose that idea on you. Rather, to love and preserve the uniqueness of your race as one among other racial subspecies of the human race is to celebrate the beauty and dignity of God's creative diversity within the human family.

Source: Hycel B. Taylor II, *The African-American Revolt of the Spirit* (Chicago: Faith and Freedom, 1996), 17.

For More Information

Helpful surveys of religion in the African American community include C. Eric Lincoln and Lawrence H. Mamiya, *The Black Church in the African-American Experience* (Durham: Duke University Press, 1990); Aminah Beverly McCloud, *African American Islam* (New York: Routledge, 1995); Richard Brent Turner, *Islam in the African-American Experience* (Bloomington: Indiana University Press, 1997); and Larry G. Murphy, ed., *Down by the Riverside: Readings in African American Religion* (New York: New York University Press, 2000). Notable works by African American Christian theologians include James H. Cone, *Risks of Faith: The Emergence of a Black Theology of Liberation, 1968–1998* (Boston: Beacon, 1999), and the video by Cornel West, "African-American Theology in Today's Society" (West Lafayette: Purdue University Public Affairs Video Archives, 1999).

The *Final Call*, the official news publication of the Nation of Islam, is available electronically at http://www.finalcall.com and in printed format by subscription from Final Call Inc., 734 W. 79th Street, Chicago, IL 60620; 773-602-1230. Mosque Maryam, the Nation of Islam's main center, is located at 7351 S. Stoney Island Avenue, Chicago, IL 60649; 773-324-6000; http://www.noi.org/maryam.html.

The title of Rev. Dr. Hycel B. Taylor II's book is *The African-American Revolt of the Spirit* (Chicago: Faith and Freedom, 1996). His thirty-year social ministry at Second Baptist Church in Evanston, Illinois (1972–2002), is examined by sociologist Shayne Lee, "The Church of Faith and Freedom: African-American Baptists and Social Action," *Journal for the Scientific Study of Religion* 42(1) (March 2003): 31–41. The phrase "faith and freedom" derives from white Christian theologian Schubert M. Ogden, *Faith and Freedom: Toward a Theology of Liberation* (Nashville: Abingdon, 1979), which was required reading in Dr. Taylor's Church and the Black Experience program at Garrett Evangelical Theological Seminary (1969–1985).

Park Manor Christian Church (Disciples of Christ), Rev. James L. Demus III's church, is located at 600 E. 73rd Street, Chicago, IL 60619; 773-483-2115; http://www.parkmanorchristianchurch. com. A transcript of the PBS story on the Million Man March, in which Rev. Demus was quoted, can be accessed at http://www. pbs.org/newshour/bb/race_relations/race_relations_10–13a.html. In addition, Rev. Demus's article, "Black Christians Encounter Black Muslims," appeared in the *Christian Ministry* (November/December 1996): 18–19.

The Web site for Matthew House is http://www.matthewhousechicago.org.

For Discussion

1. How important are religious truth claims, such as claims about God, divine revelation, the human condition, and eternal salvation? Some

Christians see them as essential in relating to the world's religions, whereas others give priority to matters like social cooperation. Where do you stand?

2. If there is a "theology of the African American experience," is there also a "theology of the white experience," a "theology of the Hispanic experience," a "theology of the Asian experience," and so on? In other words, do a group's social context and history shape its expression of Christianity, as well as its understanding of God and God's activity in the world? Is there a "theology of the human experience" shared by everyone, or are the differences in the various racial and ethnic groups' experiences more powerful than their common humanity?

3. Do you think that the rise of a new religious conservatism among younger African American Christians (mentioned by Dr. Hycel Taylor) indicates a major shift? Will "Jesiology," which sees only one way to salvation, begin to overshadow interreligious cooperation, which downplays differences in religious truth claims? What does it say about the experience of young African American conservatives that they seem to share so much with the larger, white conservative Christian movement?

4. Peruse the Web sites of Park Manor Christian Church (http://www.park-manorchristianchurch.com) and Mosque Maryam (http://www.noi.org/maryam.html), and compare and contrast them along two lines: (a) their religious truth claims and (b) their responses to the African American experience. Then compare and contrast your own religious truth claims and experience to these Web sites.

5. Minister Louis Farrakhan and the Nation of Islam are well known and controversial. What did you know about them before reading this chapter? What do you think about them now? What do you think about the Christian pastors and churches who collaborate with Minister Farrakhan and the Nation of Islam on community concerns? Would your pastor and your church do likewise, even in principle?

6. Bible passages: A guiding passage in Dr. Hycel Taylor's household is Psalm 24:1: "The earth is the Lord's and the fullness thereof." The Reverend Sanja Stinson believes that Christians should ponder Matthew 5:43–48 (loving one's enemies and forgiving one's attackers) in the wake of September 11, 2001.

TEN

Looking Back, Ahead, and into the Eyes of Others: The Orthodox Christian Experience

THE ORTHODOX CHRISTIAN PRESENCE IN the United States dates back to eighteenth-century Alaska and increased significantly with the influx of Russian, Greek, and other ethnic Orthodox groups during the heyday of immigration in the late nineteenth and early twentieth centuries. Even so, Orthodox Christianity's contributions to America's religious life have been largely ignored, as evidenced by their omission from the title of Will Herberg's acclaimed work in the 1950s, *Protestant-Catholic-Jew*.

The Orthodox Christian experience illuminates the topic at hand in important ways. As one of our interviewees, the Very Rev. Archimandrite Demetri Kantzavelos, chancellor of the Greek Orthodox Metropolis of Chicago, pointed out in our first conversation, western Christians in the United States think the issue of interreligious relations is something new, but many eastern Christians have lived as minorities in the Old World for centuries. The lessons they have learned about religious diversity deserve a hearing by all Christians.

Where shall we begin in giving a brief overview of Orthodox Christian history and interreligious relations? Orthodox Christians themselves start with the beginning of the Christian Church at the outpouring of the Holy Spirit upon the apostles at Pentecost.

When the Emperor Constantine, in the early fourth century, established Christianity as the official religion of the Roman Empire and Constantinople (ancient Byzantium) as its capital, eastern Christianity embarked upon an evolutionary trajectory in worship, doctrine, authority, and polity that differed from that of western Christianity, centered in Rome. In the Middle Ages the two eventually split for religious (see sidebar 10.1) and other reasons, and the sacking of Constantinople by western Crusaders in 1204 marked the culmination of the break.

The geographical spread of Islam, which began in the seventh century, affected Orthodox Christianity more immediately

---

SIDEBAR 10.1
The *Filioque* Controversy

Father Elias Bouboutsis, a Greek Orthodox scholar and faculty member at DePaul University in Chicago, pointed out the implications for a Christian view of other religions found in the ancient controversy between the western (Catholic) Church and the eastern (Orthodox) Church over the *filioque* clause in the Nicene-Constantinopolitan Creed, one of the contributing factors to the split that occurred in the Middle Ages. The western Church amended the original wording, "[the Holy Spirit] proceeds from the Father," to read "proceeds from the Father *and the Son* [filioque in Latin]."

"What it does," Fr. Elias explained, "is subordinate the Spirit. And what it does, furthermore, is say that the Spirit operates in the world only through the Son, through Jesus, through the Church.... This blocks the Spirit of God from acting outside the Church, which is complete arrogance to imagine that we could even say such a thing or much less do it. But not having this doctrinal limitation makes us [Orthodox Christians] step back and say, 'We can't say. We don't know. God's Spirit goes where God's Spirit wants. It doesn't have to only operate through the Church.'"

than western Christianity. Islamic rule was established in the Middle East, Asia Minor (Constantinople fell in 1453), and parts of southern Europe. Christian communities were legally protected by their Islamic rulers in deference to their religious status as People of the Book (along with Jews), but they were accorded second-class social and political status. Even so, Orthodox Christianity fared relatively well under Islam, according to some measures. As Orthodox historian Timothy Ware writes in *The Orthodox Church* (1997), "The Muslims in the fifteenth century were far more tolerant towards Christianity than western Christians were towards one another during the Reformation and the seventeenth century." We also recall the sacking of Orthodox Constantinople by western Crusaders in the thirteenth century.

Orthodox communities continue to this day in predominantly Muslim lands. The Patriarchate of Constantinople, which enjoys a special prestige among the various autocephalous (self-governing) Orthodox churches, is still located in Istanbul, Turkey (ancient Constantinople). The patriarchates of Alexandria, Antioch, and Jerusalem and the Church of Albania serve constituencies in many Muslim countries.

When it comes to interreligious relations, Orthodox Christianity draws from its past, yet also looks beyond it to see what that experience may offer for the future. According to noted Orthodox scholar Fr. Alexander Schmemann, who came to the United States in the early 1900s, "The true orthodox way of thought has always been historical, has always included the past, but has never been enslaved by it."

This sentiment was echoed by Fr. Elias Bouboutsis, the Greek Orthodox scholar and professor cited in sidebar 10.1. The Orthodox past has generated "very strong emotional ties," Fr. Elias explained, "some of which are healthy, some of which are toxic—like nationalism, which is the primary toxin in the Orthodox community today." Such nationalistic Orthodoxy has contributed to numerous interreligious and interethnic conflicts (it is difficult to separate religion and ethnicity in these contexts), like those between Orthodox Greeks and Muslim Turks or between Orthodox Serbs and Muslim Bosnians.

Father Elias has both Orthodox Christian and Muslim students who show little patience with the hatreds of the past. When they study their intersecting histories, these students, who are active in their respective local parishes and mosques, ask, "Why do my parents hate so much?" From such questions, Fr. Elias concludes, "I think things are getting much better. I think this generation is just tired of it and doesn't want it any more."

When we asked him to summarize his own views about the Orthodox Christian approach to other religions, Fr. Elias offered the notion of "reclaiming our history and disarming our history at the same time." So often in Orthodox history, the issue has been one of survival as a minority group, but he sees a promising movement "from survival to discovery." Encounters that began in conflict carry the potential for redemptive mutual understanding. Take, for example, the relationship between the Greeks and the Turks (whose respective cultures are "mirror images of the Aegean," as Fr. Elias put it), which is entering a period of redemptive discovery both abroad and in Chicago.

Father Elias was referring to local dialogues between the two communities that began in conflict on the pages of the *Chicago Tribune*. In March of 2003 Fr. Demetri Kantzavelos of the Greek Orthodox Metropolis of Chicago wrote a letter to the editor criticizing a story on ABC-TV's *Good Morning, America* program. The story featured the culture and history of Istanbul as a backdrop to America's efforts to use Turkey as a base of operations for the invasion of neighboring Iraq.

"They completely ignored the Orthodox history," Fr. Demetri explained to us. "They completely forgot to mention that it was called Constantinople when it was founded. They didn't say who founded it. They didn't even mention the [Orthodox] ecumenical base structure that was there. It was the equivalent of going to Rome and not mentioning the Vatican." For Orthodox Christians worldwide, who consider modern Turkey their ancestral ethnic and/or religious homeland, the program was "offensive," Fr. Demetri wrote in his letter to the *Tribune*. In effect, *Good Morning, America* had "dismiss[ed] the sensitivities of millions of people here and abroad by repeating politically revised history."

A week later, the *Tribune* published a response to Fr. Demetri by Mr. Mehmet Celebi, president of the local Turkish American Cultural Alliance and vice president of the Midwestern branch of the Assembly of Turkish American Associations. "Kantzavelos is still living in a dream that the Greek Empire will once again rise," wrote Mr. Celebi. He continued:

> Nobody in Turkey today denies the existence of the greatness of the civilizations that once existed in what is Turkey today.... Turkey has been and is a country comprising many cultures, ethnic groups and religions. Contrary to Kantzavelos' claim, it was the great tolerance and understanding of different religions and cultures that allowed the [Muslim] Ottoman Empire to prosper and rule over 40 different ethnic groups for 700 years.

In concluding his letter, Mr. Celebi offered some advice to Fr. Demetri and other religious leaders: "With all due respect, I urge Kantzavelos to stick to the teaching of religion and tolerance and discourage hatred and division. America and the world can only survive with the promotion of tolerance, understanding and peace. And the religious leaders of the world have a great role to play, especially in these critical times."

Mehmet Celebi shared with us some of his motivations for writing this response to Fr. Demetri's letter. "Greeks have been here [in the United States] for at least 150 years....So they grew up part of the system. We have very prominent Greek Americans: senators, congressmen, judges, etc., etc., a vice presidential candidate, a presidential candidate. And our [Turkish American] aspiration has always been for us to reach a level playing field, so we can become ourselves."

For his part, Fr. Demetri was taken aback by Mr. Celebi's letter. He immediately called Rev. Stanley Davis Jr., executive director of the Chicago and Northern Illinois Region of the National Conference for Community and Justice (formerly the National Conference of Christians and Jews), and said, "Stan, you have to find this man. I have to meet with him. He totally misunderstood me." It took a few months, but Rev. Davis finally put them in touch with one another.

"This was a good opportunity when Fr. Demetri contacted me," Mr. Celebi told us. "I said I was always open to this kind of dialogue, and I would love the opportunity to sit down and speak with him and any other way we can improve things. . . . We hit it off pretty good, actually. Since then we've become very good friends. I can always call him, and he calls me."

Father Demetri recalled that initial phone conversation:

> I started by saying that I'd like to talk about what we can
> do as communities to get past this in our history, to see if
> we can get together. I wanted to talk about the letters. He
> said, "I want to talk about the letters." . . . So then a series of
> meetings happened, and we became great friends. And now
> we're doing all sorts of work together to try to build bridges of
> understanding between our communities because historically
> we've been at odds.

That has been the pattern of interreligious relations in Chicago, according to Fr. Demetri: "An event or something triggers a response, and we begin relations. It's always issue oriented."

An important example of building bridges of understanding between Chicago's Greek and Turkish communities took place at the 2003 Dialog Dinner. This annual event, sponsored by Niagara Educational Services, an organization inspired by the life and work of Turkish philosopher and spiritual teacher M. Fethullah Gulen, doubled as both an interreligious gathering and a Muslim *iftar* dinner, the daily breaking of the fast during the month of Ramadan. Father Demetri, the first Greek Orthodox speaker ever invited to this event, apologized to the other faith traditions represented in the audience for his intention to address the historic Greek-Turkish relationship: "The Greek Orthodox and Turkish Muslim communities share a unique past; hence, I focus this evening on the complex and at times painful history that Orthodox Christianity and Islam, Greece and Turkey have suffered and shared."

He continued: "I, a Greek Orthodox priest, one born in the United States, whose spiritual ties are to that great city on the shores of the Bosphorus [Istanbul/Constantinople], stand before a primarily Turkish audience, an honored guest at a table laden with

the true food of human *being*—of human existence: understanding, mutual respect, and hope." Reflecting on their interwoven
past as Orthodox Christian Greeks and Muslim Turks, Fr. Demetri
suggested that "What we did not understand was that we were
suffering together. In retrospect (and likely into the future), our
shared history contains hope for our shared destiny." Their proxim-
ity in America offered both communities a promising opportunity:

> Time and the tides of numerous historical fortunes have
> brought us to this moment. We find ourselves here this evening
> in the United States. And we are together at this moment in
> ways that could have only occurred because of this culture's
> strengths. Imagine what this gathering might mean to our
> ancestors if they were to see our presence here this evening!
> Turks and Greeks together, sharing freedom, sharing a meal,
> sharing most importantly, hope for a still better future.

The Orthodox community in Chicago has been active for many
years in both ecumenical Christian and interreligious circles. The
Greek Orthodox Metropolis of Chicago has taken the lead in this,
for instance, by working closely with the National Conference
for Community and Justice, the Council of Religious Leaders of
Metropolitan Chicago, the American Jewish Committee, and the
Council of Islamic Organizations of Greater Chicago, in addition to
supplying a host committee for the 1993 Parliament of the World's
Religions (see the introduction to this book). In the tense atmosphere immediately following the events of September 11, 2001,
the Greek Orthodox Metropolis collaborated with the local Sikh
and Muslim communities in preparing a training video on airport
security for the Chicago Police Department. Such efforts are rooted
in deeply held values of Orthodox Christianity (see sidebar 10.2).

In his address at the 2003 Dialog Dinner, Fr. Demetri said,
"My friends, tonight we have an opportunity to look at each other
in a unique and intense way, and, seeing one another in truth and
love, we may yet see ourselves in the other." He went on to quote
a favorite phrase of Ecumenical Patriarch Athenagoras, who held
the honored throne of the Patriarchate of Constantinople from
1948 to 1972 and was a tireless proponent of Christian ecumenical

---

SIDEBAR 10.2
Statement from the Orthodox Christian Community of Chicago

The world community of Orthodox Churches (numbering over 250,000,000) has been an active participant in the ecumenical movement since its beginnings. Their leaders have for decades demonstrated a deep commitment to dialogues of truth and love, valuing respect, honesty, and cooperation among the followers of all religions. Embracing the ethos of the Ecumenical Patriarch of Constantinople, the Orthodox seek to grow in understanding of different faith traditions as a first step toward fulfilling Christ's own prayer, "That they may all be one." (John 17:21)

Source: *2006 InterFaith Calendar,* published by the National Conference for Community and Justice of Chicago and Greater Illinois.

---

and interreligious dialogue and harmony: "Come let us look into one another's eyes." Father Demetri elaborated with a lesson on the Greek language: "We know that we exist as people—the word I want to use is 'persons.' We know that we are persons because of other persons." The Greek roots of the word "person" include the word for "side" or "face." "So, a person is a person when he or she comes face to face with another person." The same holds for peoples, that is, collective persons. When they encounter each other face to face and look into one another's eyes, they can discover their full humanity together.

Like Orthodoxy generally, Fr. Demetri reaches back to the ancient authorities of the Church for guidance in reaching out to others today. "When we act with non-Orthodox and non-Christians, we have a sense of ourselves and an understanding of how to reach out. We also have a theological underpinning for doing social justice and activism based on writings of the Church Fathers. Basil the Great spoke about social justice. During the Byzantine period he established outreach programs, hospitals, orphanages, and places for women.... When we engage in such work, we are acting upon our historical identity."

"There's an ancient authenticity that we proclaim, based on Church values and history," Fr. Demetri said of Orthodox Christianity. "It sounds so fresh and new—and so modern, which I think is great. But it's also timeless."

For More Information

Will Herberg's acclaimed, though flawed, portrait of the mid-twentieth-century American religious landscape is *Protestant-Catholic-Jew: An Essay in American Religious Sociology* (Garden City, N.Y.: Doubleday, 1955). In a footnote, Herberg logs the lament of Orthodox Christians that they are the forgotten Fourth Great Faith of America. On this, see Charles C. Moskos, "The Greek Orthodox Church in America," in *Reading Greek America: Studies in the Experience of Greeks in the United States,* ed. Spyros D. Orfanos (New York: Pella, 2002), 85–98.

Two helpful articles on the Web site of the Greek Orthodox Archdiocese of America are Aristeides Papadakis, "History of the Orthodox Church," http://www.goarch.org/en/ourfaith/articles/article7053.asp, and George C. Papademetriou, "An Orthodox Reflection on Truth and Tolerance," http://www.goarch.org/en/ourfaith/articles/article8075.asp. Comprehensive scholarly books on Orthodox Christianity include Alexander Schmemann, *The Historical Road of Eastern Orthodoxy*, trans. Lydia W. Kesich (New York: Holt, Rinehart and Winston, 1963); Timothy Ware, *The Orthodox Church*, new ed. (New York: Penguin, 1997); Kallistos Ware, *The Orthodox Way* (Crestwood, N.Y.: St. Vladimir's Seminary Press, 1995); and Jaroslav Pelikan, *The Spirit of Eastern Christendom (600–1700)* (Chicago: University of Chicago Press, 1977).

The Orthodox Church in America represents Russian, Romanian, Albanian, and Bulgarian Orthodox churches in the United States (P.O. Box 675, Syosset, N.Y. 11791-0675; phone 516-922-

0550; http://www.oca.org). The Web site for the Greek Orthodox Archdiocese of America is http://www.goarch.org; the contact information for the Greek Orthodox Metropolis of Chicago, where Fr. Demetri Kantzavelos serves as chancellor, is 40 E. Burton Place, Chicago IL 60610-1697, phone 312-337-4130; http://www.chicago.goarch.org.

A transcript of the address given by Fr. Demetri Kantzavelos at the 2003 Dialog Dinner is available on the Web site of Zaman Online: First Turkish Paper on the Internet, http://www.zaman.com/?bl=showcase&alt=&hn=4511. Father Demetri supplied us with a printed copy of the address. For information about M. Fethullah Gulen, the Turkish philosopher and spiritual teacher cited by Fr. Demetri in his talk, go to http://www.fethullahgulen.org. The contact information for the Turkish American Cultural Alliance, where Mr. Mehmet Celebi serves as president, is 3845 N. Harlem Avenue, Chicago, IL 60634; phone 509-695-1487; email taca@tacaonline.org; http://www.tacaonline.org/CMS.

The National Conference for Community and Justice has once again changed its name and now calls itself the Chicago Center for Cultural Connections. Its contact information is 27 E. Monroe Street, Suite 400, Chicago, IL 60603; phone 312-236-9272; http://www.connections-chicago.org.

For Discussion

1. In his address at the Dialog Dinner, Fr. Demetri Kantzavelos, chancellor of the Greek Orthodox Metropolis of Chicago, quoted these words from Turkish philosopher and spiritual teacher' M. Fethullah Gulen: "Negative feelings and attributes often defeat people, pulling them under their domination to such an extent that even the religions that guide people to goodness and kindness are abused, as well as the feelings and attributes that are sources of absolute good." Discuss the role of religions in both combating and contributing to the "negative feelings and attributes" that often defeat individuals and groups.

2. In his address, Fr. Demetri spoke directly to the Greek Orthodox and Turkish Muslim communities in Chicago. Reflect on his words: "We find ourselves here this evening in the United States. And we are together at this moment in ways that could have only occurred because of this culture's strengths. Imagine what this gathering might mean to our ancestors if they were to see our presence here this evening!" What strengths are found in American culture that can help to overcome historical tensions among ethnic and religious groups?

3. If you are not an Orthodox Christian, what did you know about Orthodox Christianity before reading this chapter? Summarize Orthodoxy's perspectives on non-Christian religions that other Christians might fruitfully consider. Peruse the Orthodox Web sites listed under "For More Information" in this chapter for examples of the "ancient authenticity that we proclaim, based on Church values and history," as Fr. Demetri put it. In what ways might Orthodoxy sound fresh, new, modern, and yet timeless?

4. One of our interviewees complained about Christian groups that do not recognize the validity of Orthodox Christianity. "They do not even consider us Christians," he told us. "We're pagans, we're some weird thing, and we don't count in their calculus. There's an Orthodox Church of Iraq that's two thousand years old, and they're sending people over there to evangelize them." Discuss the ways in which Christians define the boundaries of the Christian faith, thus defining non-Christians as "others." Where do you draw the boundaries, and how do you approach the "others" outside those boundaries?

5. Recall the Orthodox Christian delegation's withdrawal from the 1993 Parliament of the World's Religions in protest over the presence of groups "which profess no belief in God or a supreme being" and "certain quasi-religious groups with which Orthodox Christians share no common ground" (see the introduction to this book). Discuss that decision in light of this chapter.

6. Bible passages: A report on a 2007 meeting in Jerusalem between Jewish and Orthodox Christian representatives, titled "Communique of the 6th Academic Meeting between Judaism and Orthodox

Christianity" (http://www.ec-patr.org/docdisplay.php?lang=en&id= 769&tla=en), cites Genesis 1:26–27 (human beings created in the image of God) as a basis for respecting and protecting the fundamental human right of religious freedom. "Holy Pasha 2008," an encyclical by the patriarch of Alexandria (http://www. greekorthodox-alexandria.org/index.php?module=content&action =details&cid=001004&id=212), reflects on the peace and good-will offered to all in Christ's Resurrection. Consider the following New Testament chapters regarding the Resurrection: Matthew 28, Ephesians 1, and Colossians 1.

ELEVEN

More Hindus and Others Come to Town

WE LEFT THE CHURCHES OF Aurora, Illinois, in chapter 1. The arrival of Sri Venkateswara Swami Temple of Greater Chicago in the mid-1980s created a stirring public debate among Aurora Christians, who took three basic positions regarding the theological and civic issues raised by the new Hindu presence in town. Some sought to prevent the erection of the Hindu temple altogether by claiming a biblical mandate to oppose idolatry. Others recognized the Hindu community's legal right to build a temple in Aurora but also viewed the temple's membership as a missionary field for Christian evangelization. The third camp welcomed the temple as a symbol of religious diversity and felt no need to evangelize its members, seeing it rather as an opportunity to learn more about Hinduism, as well as their own Christian faith.

Chapter 1 ended by noting that the reconsecration of the Sri Venkateswara temple in 2003, fully covered by the local newspaper, stimulated no public response, in contrast to the controversy nearly twenty years earlier. This chapter examines the current situation in Aurora more closely, explores the city's new religious diversity, and revisits the principal churches involved in the 1985 debate to see what they are doing in this regard today.

The U.S. Census Bureau's 2006 estimate placed Aurora as the second largest city in the state of Illinois (behind Chicago), with more than 170,000 residents. Aurora's historic racial and ethnic minorities, African Americans and Hispanics, now make up a large percentage of the city's total population, while the Asian population has increased noticeably in recent years, with Indians as the largest Asian subgroup.

Since the census does not ask questions about religious affiliation, the contours of Aurora's religious diversity are a bit more speculative. Christians clearly compose the majority religious group in the area, although the precise boundaries of the Christian fold are a matter of debate among the faithful. The listing under "churches" in the *Yellow Pages* for greater Aurora stretches for ten pages and includes dozens of Baptist churches, a page of Lutherans, more than a page of nondenominational churches, and myriad other kinds of Protestant congregations. The listing also includes nearly forty Roman Catholic parishes, three Byzantine Catholic churches, seven congregations from the Mormon tradition, four Jehovah's Witnesses Kingdom Halls, four Christian Science groups, three Orthodox Christian churches, and two Unitarian Universalist congregations—all considered non-Christian by some of the Protestants we interviewed for this book. The non-Christian representatives in greater Aurora that everyone can agree upon include two Jewish synagogues, two Baha'i local spiritual assemblies, three Muslim mosques, and several Buddhist and Hindu groups.

We discussed two of the mosques in the Aurora area in chapter 4, Batavia Islamic Center, which meets in the basement of Calvary Episcopal Church, and Fox Valley Muslim Community Center, which built a new facility in Aurora in the early 1990s. The latter drew local news coverage when it opened—but no public debate. Some of our interviewees speculated that the controversy over the Sri Venkateswara Hindu temple just a few years earlier may have muted public discourse about the new mosque. Perhaps people had wearied of the topic. Perhaps Islam, as a monotheistic religion with a historical relationship to Judaism and Christianity, was perceived by most Aurora Christians at the time (pre-September 11, 2001) as less different in key ways than Hinduism.

Several Hindu and Hindu-influenced groups have joined the Sri Venkateswara temple in the greater Aurora area since the mid-1980s. A center for Transcendental Meditation, the movement made famous in the 1960s by Maharishi Mahesh Yogi, is planned near the local shopping mall. Followers of the Arya Samaj Hindu reform movement meet in West Chicago, a town just north of Aurora. A large BAPS Swaminarayan temple, a small Yog Sadhan Ashram facility, and a mid-sized Swadhyah congregation are located farther north, while a Siddha Yoga chanting group gathers regularly in Naperville, Aurora's neighbor to the east. Just a short distance from the Sri Venkateswara temple, a second Aurora Hindu temple, Sri Shirdi Sai Baba Mandir Chicago, was built in 2006 by followers of Sri Shirdi Sai Baba, whom they revere as both religious teacher and divine manifestation. Local newspaper coverage of this new temple drew no public response, just as with the reconsecration of the Sri Venkateswara temple in 2003. In 2007 the Chicago-area branch of Bharat Sevashram Sangha of North America became Aurora's third Hindu temple, occupying a former Christian Science church. This group, headquartered in India, was founded in 1917 by Swami Pranavanandaji Maharaj, whom they also revere as both religious teacher and divine incarnation. See sidebar 11.1 for a brief overview of the diversity within Hinduism.

We contacted the principal churches involved in the 1985 public debate about Aurora's first Hindu temple. Most have not pursued the issue of Aurora's growing religious diversity in any systematic way since that time.

Recall the strong statements by Rev. and Mrs. John Riggs of Union Congregational Church in chapter 1. Despite recognizing the local Hindu community's civic right to build a temple, Rev. Riggs granted the truth claims of Hinduism no quarter. In addition, Mrs. Riggs feared God's judgment on both Aurora and the nation for allowing an idolatrous presence in the land and abandoning America's Christian foundations. Today, Union Congregational Church "isn't doing a blessed thing" specifically on the topic of local religious diversity, according to a church leader. The congregation focuses its energies on strengthening its own spiritual health rather than addressing external issues. However, church leaders do encourage members to witness to neighbors and acquaintances, which may include adherents of other faiths.

The two churches located within a few hundred yards of the Sri Venkateswara temple in Aurora have changed identities since 1985.

SIDEBAR 11.1
Hindu Diversity

The diversity within Hinduism rivals that within Christianity. Hindu immigrants and American converts practice a wide variety of religious subtraditions in the United States. A major distinction has to do with how divinity is worshiped: Some Hindu groups focus on gods and goddesses represented by images, while others revere living gurus or spiritual teachers believed to manifest divinity in their lives.

The three Hindu temples in Aurora, Illinois, illustrate these diverse approaches. Sri Venkateswara Swami Temple of Greater Chicago houses ten images of Hindu deities, of which the temple's patron deity is Sri Venkateswara (also called Balaji), a south Indian variation of the major Hindu god, Vishnu. The other two temples revere their spiritual founders as living manifestations of the divine: Sri Shirdi Sai Baba, born ca. 1835 in central India, and Swami Pranavanandaji Maharaj, founder of Bharat Sevashram Sangha, born in 1896 in Bangladesh.

Souls Harbor Open Bible Church is now River of Life Christian Center. Local religious diversity is not a major concern for the new church. Mustard Seed Tabernacle Bible Church, an African American congregation, disbanded not long after the Hindu temple controversy of the 1980s.

Westminster Presbyterian Church (USA), which organized a seminar series on Hinduism in the 1980s, has no comparable programming today. A congregational leader told us about his stance on the Southern Baptist Convention's intention to send evangelists to witness to the non-Christians of the Chicago area in the summer of 2000. He criticized the letter sent by the Council of Religious Leaders of Metropolitan Chicago to the Southern Baptist Convention, which asked the Baptists to call off their crusade. A Presbyterian official involved in the controversy explained to him that the Baptists had made it sound like the Presbyterians do not evangelize. "Well, then, what is the denomination doing?" he asked the official, but he feels he did not receive a straight answer to his lament over the Presbyterians' evangelical apathy.

In 1985 Rev. Clara Thompson of First Baptist Church wrote a letter to the editor of the local newspaper deploring prejudice against Hindus and supporting the Hindu community's presence in the city. According to a congregational leader, there has been no discussion of Hindus or Hinduism at First Baptist Church for years. The church offered one adult Sunday school session on Islam after the events of September 11, 2001, but that has been the extent of its programming on world religions.

Only two churches involved in the 1980s' controversy have devoted significant time or thought to the topic of Aurora's growing religious diversity and have taken very different approaches. Both New England Congregational Church and Orchard Valley Community Church find opportunity here but do not define it in the same way.

New England Congregational Church: "The More, the Merrier"

New England Congregational Church, a United Church of Christ (UCC) congregation, played a relatively minor role in the controversy over the new Aurora Hindu temple in the 1980s. The church organized an adult study class on Hinduism, which took a field trip to the Sri Venkateswara temple when it opened. As the church's current senior minister, Rev. Gary McCann, explained to us, New England Church wanted to make a "welcoming statement" in contrast to those Christians who alternatively feared the new Hindu presence in town, wished to keep it out, or saw it as an opportunity to evangelize. A few years later the church organized another adult education class, which brought in a Hindu speaker and took another field trip to the temple. Through these initiatives, New England Church invited local Hindus to educate them about Hinduism and let the Hindu community know that the church celebrated their unique contribution to Aurora's religious diversity. This approach was consistent with the church's self-identity as an open and inclusive congregation vis-à-vis all groups. Recalling the overwhelming response by members who participated in the two adult study classes, Rev. McCann stated that it was one of pleasant surprise at the parallels between Christianity and Hinduism. "Wow, I believe that, too!" was often heard after discussions of Hindu tenets.

Of all of the churches involved in the 1980s' controversy, New England Church has sustained the most interest in the topic of religious diversity and has incorporated it into its programming in a variety of ways. Over the years, the church has had a close relationship with the Aurora synagogue, Temple B'nai Israel, such as participating in joint worship services. In response to the events of September 11, 2001, Hamid and Mazher Ahmed, founders of Batavia Islamic Center (see chapter 4), represented Islam in two commemorative services at New England Church. The Youth Ministries program is intentional about studying other religions and takes field trips to local non-Christian religious sites. The program's Web site features the motto adopted by the youth: the Golden Rule as expressed in seven world religions (Buddhism, Christianity, Confucianism, Hinduism, Islam, Judaism, and Taoism).

Sunday morning worship services at New England Church regularly incorporate readings and ideas from non-Christian religions. Some members of his congregation, says Rev. McCann, gave him the idea of pairing scriptural texts from other religions with biblical texts as the basis for his sermons, which draws upon the approach of a UCC pastor in Wisconsin. Perusing the sermon archives on New England Church's Web site reveals Rev. McCann's preference for the Bhagavad Gita (Hinduism), the Tao-te Ching (Taoism), and the Qur'an (Islam), with occasional selections from devotional writers like Khalil Gibran and Thich Nhat Hanh. The sermon we heard during our site visit drew from Genesis and the Tao-te Ching (see number 6 under "For Discussion" at the end of this chapter). Besides the passage that was read aloud from the Tao-te Ching, the worship service overall, including the sermon, made only subtle references to Taoist ideas.

This understated approach to other religions, what associate minister Rev. Joe Dunham calls "respectful recognition," typifies New England Church. Although church leaders and most of the members are self-consciously liberal on social, political, and theological issues, their liberalism is not aggressively paraded in an in-your-face manner, which would offend conservative members, according to Rev. McCann. The first half of the church's motto, "A Caring Church for Thinking People," emphasizes the importance of the bonds of Christian community within the congregation, while the second half emphasizes free thinking without dogmatism, whether liberal or conservative. For Rev. McCann, the biblical testimonies of Jesus and Paul challenge the boundaries that people set for themselves with regard to both caring and thinking, thereby pushing the envelope of people's openness to other groups and ideas. He applies the parable of the Good Samaritan to today's Hindus, Muslims, and other non-Christians.

We observed a bit of New England Church's respectful openness to internal congregational diversity during our visit. A statement in the worship bulletin read: "Please use the gender language most meaningful for your worship experience." During the singing of the doxology, some of the worshipers followed the gender-neutral text printed in the bulletin, but most sang the traditional masculine words. Underlying the resulting lyrical disharmony one could detect a communal unity, where liberal and conservative Christians have created a comfortable space for each other in worship.

Associate minister Dunham chairs the philosophy department at nearby Aurora University. Raised a Southern Baptist, he finds New England Church's embrace of religious diversity "a breath of fresh air." He attributes the relatively harmonious coexistence of theological liberals and conservatives in the congregation to the absence of an overly prescriptive creed. For instance, the church's statement, titled "We believe," includes self-identification as a "theologically liberal" congregation, but it also states, "We believe in the teaching of the Gospel variously interpreted in a non-creedal environment." According to Rev. Dunham, those conservatives who feel too uncomfortable with the liberal aspects of the church usually take their membership elsewhere.

In his sermons, Rev. Dunham chooses not to draw from the scriptures of other religions. "It's too risky," he told us, "especially if taken out of context. I may be misusing the texts." His approach to other religions is based on inclusive New Testament passages, such as Jesus' mention of "other sheep" in John 10, and the school of process theology, derived from philosopher Alfred North Whitehead, which proposes an inclusive God. The Reverend Dunham feels quite comfortable with New England Church's approach. As he put it, "we affirm the possibility of meeting the divine, or God, in a variety of ways and settings."

One member of New England Church is Dr. Martin Forward, executive director of Aurora University's Wackerlin Center for Faith and Action. Just days after 9/11, Dr. Forward preached a sermon there, titled "God in a World of Christians and Muslims," which drew upon his long association with Muslims in England, India, and the Middle East. He and Rev. McCann have discussed the possibility of establishing a local parliament of religious leaders, including the priests of the Sri Venkateswara Hindu temple and the imam of Fox Valley Muslim Community Center in Aurora.

We asked Rev. McCann for his thoughts on Sri Shirdi Sai Baba Mandir Chicago, one of the new Hindu temples in town. "The more, the merrier," he replied without hesitation. "Diversity always enhances who we are as communities of faith. If your faith is strong, diversity will not threaten it." Moreover, Rev. McCann also feels that Aurora churches should educate people about new and unfamiliar religious groups in order to avoid a repeat of the misinformation about Hinduism that circulated during the controversy over the Sri Venkateswara temple in the 1980s.

Orchard Valley Community Church: "The Greatest Opportunity That We Have Ever Had"

Here is the paragraph from chapter 1 that describes the position of the pastor of our second Aurora congregation regarding the Sri Venkateswara temple in 1985, drawn from his letter to the editor of the local newspaper:

> The pastor of Aurora First Assembly of God, Rev. Larry
> Hodge, characterized himself both as "an American who

cherishes freedom and as a Christian who serves the Christ."
With respect to the first point, "As long as the owners of [the
Hindu temple] meet the legal requirements for construction,
they should be allowed to build whatever they choose." With
respect to the second point, wrote Rev. Hodge, "I must stand
in opposition to the teaching and practices the owners of
this property will bring to this community. Their teaching
and practices produce no real spiritual hope or lasting social
redemption." Come what may, Rev. Hodge pledged "to
proclaim Jesus Christ as the only hope for this world and its
inhabitants."

In the years following the 1980s' Hindu temple controversy,
First Assembly of God changed its name to Orchard Valley
Community Church and built an impressive new facility on the
outskirts of Aurora. Soon after settling in there, Rev. Hodge had
a spiritual "encounter" with God that led him to shift the congregation's focus toward reaching out to the unchurched masses of
Aurora, which Rev. Hodge estimated to be 85 percent of the total
population on any given Sunday. The church adopted a "seeker
sensitive" approach inspired in large part by the Willow Creek
Community Church model. Willow Creek is the renowned megachurch in South Barrington, Illinois, which promotes innovative
worship and programming through its Willow Creek Association,
to which Orchard Valley Community Church belongs.

During our interview, Rev. Hodge reflected on the Hindu temple controversy and the issues it raised for Aurora Christians both
then and now.

In 1985 Aurora still had a relatively small-town, parochial identity, noted Rev. Hodge, so a proposed Hindu temple shocked many
local Christians. Although his letter to the editor (cited earlier)
focused equally on the civic and theological aspects of the situation, for Rev. Hodge the crux of the matter was the spiritual battle
unfolding behind the scenes. He saw the Hindu temple as "just
another attempt of spiritual forces to manipulate and to maneuver
and to oppose some of the free flow of the work of churches, in
particular, in Aurora. I don't mean to be simplistic about this in
my approach," he continued, "but I believe that in the nonmaterial

world there are both good and evil forces at work, and I take that view from my interpretation of scripture. And I believe, of course, that there's really no contest there, that God is creator of all and that Satan and all of his forces, after all, really were created by God."

Then Rev. Hodge went on to talk about idols, that is, anything people place between themselves and God, whether made of stone or human materials. "Behind each and every one of those idols are demonic spirits.... So when I saw the Hindu temple coming into the city of Aurora, I saw, in my opinion, an attempt of the Enemy [Satan] to move an incredible amount of his force into this city, which I already thought had enough of it anyway."

After much prayer and conversation with other Christian leaders about "the immense amount of spiritual opposition" he had always sensed in Aurora, Rev. Hodge eventually decided that the Sri Venkateswara temple was a nonissue.

"I handled it from a spiritual standpoint," he explained. "I understand spiritual warfare to the point of binding and loosing, and I simply let it go, and it's been a nonissue to me. It's just a nonissue. Now, it might be an issue as far as density and population and the look of the project [the temple facility] and all that kind of stuff, but as far as that affecting the city of Aurora and Christian testimony, Christian movement, I settled that issue. As far as I was concerned, it would never, ever be an issue."

When the Muslim mosque was built in Aurora a few years after the Hindu temple, Rev. Hodge maintained that stance, as he did at the time of our interview regarding the imminent construction of the second Hindu temple in town, Sri Shirdi Sai Baba Mandir Chicago. The presence of these non-Christian facilities is simply a spiritual nonissue for the city of Aurora in his estimation. Temples or mosques certainly could not deter him or his congregation from their mission of reaching Aurora's unchurched masses, which include Hindus, Muslims, and adherents of other non-Christian faiths. Orchard Valley Community Church has not designed any programs or activities specifically for such non-Christian groups. The church hopes to attract them the same way that it attracts other unchurched people—through personal evangelism by church members. That is how one Muslim person became a regular attendee.

In order to benefit the city of Aurora, Rev. Hodge was more than willing to collaborate with non-Christians on practical good works. For instance, his church has cosponsored a food distribution program with a local Mormon congregation (they consider Mormons to be non-Christians). He also had an especially close personal and professional relationship with a former rabbi of Aurora's synagogue, Temple B'nai Israel. The two were integral to the establishment of an interfaith counseling service for the greater Aurora area, although Rev. Hodge told the rabbi up front that he would never refer a member of his congregation to him for counseling "because you do not believe in Christ, and I believe that He is the one who changes us all."

"Probably," Rev. Hodge speculated, "if the Hindus had some big thing going on that was going to help for the overall good of the community, and we could work together in some positive way, I'd probably do that too,…for the good of humanity."

Not long before his death in 2004, we asked Rev. Hodge for his opinion about the broader significance of America's growing religious diversity, particularly through recent immigration. He acknowledged that many Christians might view this growth in a negative sense, as an unwanted challenge to Christianity. But he looked at it quite positively: "For the church of the Lord Jesus Christ, which is the body of Christ on earth, it seems to me to be the greatest opportunity that we have ever had." Alluding again to the notion of spiritual warfare, Rev. Hodge said, "I personally believe that whenever Christ is put up against anything, He wins hands down."

For More Information

Regarding Aurora's first Hindu temple, Sri Venkateswara Swami Temple of Greater Chicago, other Hindu temples in the United States, and American Hinduism generally, see "For More Information" in chapter 1. The Web site of Aurora's second Hindu temple, Sri Shirdi Sai Baba Mandir Chicago (http://www.

saisamsthanusa.org/newsite), includes a history of the local group in its "About Us" feature. The Web site of Aurora's third Hindu temple, Bharat Sevashram Sangha of North America (http://www.bharatsevashram.org), posts the minutes of its governing committee meetings, giving an inside view of the temple's work (see http://www.bharatsevashram.org/minutes.htm).

For the Southern Baptist Convention's own coverage of the controversy over their intention to send evangelists to Chicago in the summer of 2000, see the article posted on its Internet news outlet, Art Toalston, "Paige Patterson to Chicago Leaders: Baptists to Stay Focused on the City," http://www.bpnews.net/bpnews.asp?Id=3077 (November 30, 1999).

Contact information for this chapter's two featured congregations: New England Congregational Church, 406 W. Galena Boulevard, Aurora, IL 60506; 630-897-8721; e-mail office@newenglandchurch.org; http://www.newenglandchurch.org; Youth Ministries program Web site, http://www.chestnuthouse.org (featuring the Golden Rule as expressed in seven world religions); Orchard Valley Community Church, 101 Barnes Road, Aurora, IL 60506; 630-897-8888; e-mail info@orchardvalleyonline.com; http://www.orchardvalleyonline.com. Orchard Valley Community Church is a member of the Willow Creek Association, an arm of the megachurch Willow Creek Church (http://www.willowcreek.org).

The Web site for Aurora University's Wackerlin Center for Faith and Action is http://www.aurora.edu/cfa. The center's motto is "Sustaining multifaith understanding and action." The center's director, Dr. Martin Forward, has written a book titled *Inter-Religious Dialogue: A Short Introduction* (Oxford, UK: Oneworld, 2002).

For Discussion

1. Do a *Yellow Pages* or Internet search of the religious diversity in your local area. Is your area's religious diversity comparable to that of Aurora, Illinois? Is your area more diverse or less? How do you draw

the boundaries of the Christian fold? Which groups do you include, which do you exclude, and what criteria do you use in making your judgments? What implications are involved in such an identification process for interreligious relations?

2. Browse the Web sites of the Hindu temples listed under "For More Information" in this chapter. What reactions do you have in reading about Hindu beliefs and practices? As local religious organizations, how might these Hindu temples compare and contrast with your congregation on an institutional level? What do you think about the Hindu understanding of divinity, particularly the focus on human manifestations of divinity in some groups?

3. With regard to Aurora's growing religious diversity, Rev. Gary McCann of New England Congregational Church and Rev. Larry Hodge of Orchard Valley Community Church both expressed positive sentiments. Discuss their differing reasons for welcoming non-Christian groups to town. Which pastor resonates more with your views?

4. What do you make of the fact that most of the churches involved in the Aurora Hindu temple controversy of the 1980s have not pursued the issue of the area's growing religious diversity in any systematic way? The introduction to this book suggests that this fact, plus the lack of public response to the opening of Aurora's second Hindu temple, may indicate a growing willingness among Christians to grant civic accommodation to America's increasing religious diversity or at least resignation to demographic realities. Do you agree? After reading the case studies in this book, how important is America's religious diversity to you? To your congregation?

5. Bible passages: Rev. Gary McCann's August 4, 2002, sermon, "A Magnificent Defeat," draws from Genesis 32:22–31 (Jacob wrestling with God) and two verses of the Tao-te Ching (see the sermon archives of New England Congregational Church's Web site, http://www.newenglandchurch.org). The notion of spiritual warfare that Rev. Larry Hodge described is found in Ephesians 6:10–20.

Conclusion: Local Christians Face America's New Religious Diversity

A FEW YEARS AGO, WALKING along Broadway Street in Chicago, I experienced a multireligious moment that typified America's changing landscape. In front of Quan Am Tu Vietnamese Buddhist Temple, I saw a Muslim bumper sticker that said "I ♥ ALLAH."

As the introduction to this book notes, the *quantitative* markers of America's new religious diversity are not confined to major metropolises like Chicago, as new temples, mosques, and other non-Christian centers sprout up across our religious landscape. Even more important, Americans have experienced a *qualitative* shift in their self-perception as a nation and are increasingly seeing the United States as a multireligious society.

This book has described the variety of Christian responses to multireligious neighborhoods, towns, and nation. As we have seen, there is no one way that American Christians relate to their new religious neighbors. During my walk along Broadway Street in Chicago someone handed me a Christian tract titled "Heaven or Hell: Which Is for You?" Published by Fellowship Tract League of Lebanon, Ohio, the tract concluded with the statement "Jesus Christ awaits your choice" and quoted John 3:18, "He that believeth on him is not condemned: but he that believeth not is condemned already."

This is one Christian response to Buddhist temples and Muslim bumper stickers. As we have seen, however, other Christians do not see religious diversity in the United States as a matter of saving souls. Even within a single congregation, Christians disagree on how to approach other religions. The variety of responses to America's multireligious reality was typified in a Dear Abby advice column a few years ago.

Writers from Bend, Oregon; Sacramento, California; Ellijay, Georgia; Lacey, Washington; and New York City responded to "Happy Hindu in the Bible Belt," who sought Abby's advice about her Christian friends' attempts to convert her. The writers debated the appropriateness of the evangelizing efforts in terms of both theology and social etiquette. One writer explained, "You have to understand that, with evangelicals, it is an article of faith, and it's their Christian duty to preach their version of the Gospel, especially if they care about you and are genuinely concerned about your soul." Other Christian writers expressed chagrin at proselytization in principle. Abby, aka Jeanne Phillips, who is Jewish, advised that "Anyone who proselytizes is treading on 'sacred ground.' It's regarded as offensive, even if it is heartfelt."

This concluding chapter attempts first to sort out the great variety of Christian perspectives in a multireligious America, as illustrated in the case studies of this book. Does a typology or classification of types emerge here that can offer a fresh way of looking at the important topic of Christian relations with other religions? However, this chapter goes beyond mere classification to ask a crucial question of all Christians regardless of perspective: How would you wish adherents of other religions to think of you and the Christian faith?

The Variety of Christian Perspectives on Other Religions

In recent decades Christian theologians and authors have offered many typologies of Christian perspectives on other religions. Some of these are unhelpfully complex, and others deceptively simple (perhaps even unhelpfully simplistic), but all of them attempt to classify the approaches to non-Christian religions found among the many traditions, denominations, and groups making up the Christian faith. Moreover, they all recognize the growing importance of the topic. For instance, Owen C. Thomas's 1969 volume, *Attitudes toward Other Religions: Some Christian Interpretations*, presents two overlapping typologies that comprise a total of eighteen types—an example of unhelpful complexity—but his observation that other religions present "a pressing theoretical and practical issue for Christians" hits the nail on the head. Paul F. Knitter's more recent book, *Introducing Theologies of Religions*, describes four models of Christianity's place among the world's religions—replacement, fulfillment, mutuality, acceptance—through which "Christians are facing questions and challenges they never had to confront before (at least not in this intensity)."

Alan Race, in his 1983 book *Christians and Religious Pluralism: Patterns in the Christian Theology of Religions*, examines the dilemma of the modern era, brought on by new knowledge from the comparative study of religions and increasing contacts among the religious peoples of the world. A "Christian theology of religions," Race explains, seeks "to evaluate the relationship between the Christian faith and the faith of the other religions." Race proposes a threefold classification of Christian perspectives on other religions that continues to dominate the discussion despite recent criticisms of its usefulness: exclusivism, inclusivism, and pluralism.

Harvard University's Diana L. Eck discusses this typology in her 1993 spiritual autobiography, *Encountering God*. She points out that these are not the only possible perspectives and that they can be found among the followers of any religion:

> First, there is the exclusivist response: Our own community, our tradition, our understanding of reality, our encounter with God, is the one and only truth, excluding all others. Second, there is the inclusivist response: There are, indeed, many communities, traditions, and truths, but our own way of seeing things is the culmination of the others, superior to the others, or at least wide enough to include the others under our universal canopy and in our own terms. A third response is that of the pluralist: Truth is not the exclusive or inclusive possession of any one tradition or community. Therefore the diversity of communities, traditions, understandings of

the truth, and visions of God is not an obstacle for us to
overcome, but an opportunity for our energetic engagement
and dialogue with one another. It does not mean giving up our
commitments; rather, it means opening up those commitments
to the give-and-take of mutual discovery, understanding, and,
indeed, transformation.

Note how the exclusivism/inclusivism/pluralism classification
focuses on the issue of religious truth claims. Christian exclusivists, for instance, claim that Christianity represents the only truth,
Christian inclusivists claim that Christianity's truth subsumes
or fulfills other religious truths, and Christian pluralists claim
that Christianity's truth is one among many understandings of
truth. Don Pittman, Ruben Habito, and Terry Muck, in their volume *Ministry and Theology in Global Perspective: Contemporary
Challenges for the Church,* call these "theological options" and
point up the emphasis on Christian doctrines such as revelation,
sin, grace, and salvation. Employing similar typologies, other
observers have attempted to quantify the prevalence of various
types in the U.S. population (see sidebars C.1 and C.2).

This focus on religious truth claims explains a lot, and we have
certainly seen examples of exclusivists, inclusivists, and pluralists
throughout this book. Recall, for instance, the internal debate at
St. Silas Lutheran Church (chapter 5), where Pastor Jack Fischer
took an exclusivist stance in contrasting the truth claims of
Christianity with the false claims of Islam, whereas the missionary Wilton DeMast inclusively sought aspects of Islamic theology
that contain partial perceptions of the full divine revelation found
in Jesus Christ. Inclusivism also characterizes the theology of the
Second Vatican Council of the Roman Catholic Church, which
inspires parishes like St. Lambert to explore how other religions
"often reflect a ray of that Truth which enlightens all men," in
the words of *Nostra Aetate* (chapter 7). Father Michael Rasicci
of Calvary Episcopal Church (chapter 4) even used the word in
invoking what he considers the genius of the Anglican tradition:
"We call it 'inclusive' today—it used to be called 'comprehensive'—
trying to see the whole picture and where people can fit into this
whole picture of God's plan and the plan of salvation." "In some

SIDEBAR C.1
Gallup's Religious Tolerance Index

The Gallup Organization has devised an index of Americans' attitudes toward adherents of other religions. Based on the results of polls beginning in 2002, Gallup created three categories of religious tolerance: (1) *isolated*, those who "tend to believe in the truth of their perspective above all others"; (2) *tolerant*, those who take a "live-and-let-live" attitude toward other religions and are unlikely to make much effort to learn about them; and (3) *integrated*, those who go beyond the "live-and-let-live" attitude of the Tolerant category and "actively seek to know more about and learn from others of different religious traditions." The following graph shows the percentages of each category represented in the 2004 Gallup poll.

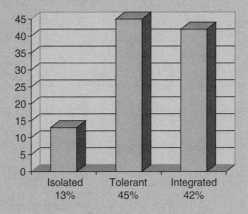

	Isolated	Tolerant	Integrated
	13%	45%	42%

Source: Albert L. Winseman, "Religious Tolerance Score Edged Up in 2004," http://www.gallup.com/poll/15253/Religious-Tolerance-Score-Edged-2004.aspx.

ways," Fr. Rasicci told us, "most of the world religions, if not all, share in parts of the truth that we would say, as Christians, we have the privilege to have in its fullness." We have also seen theological pluralism in this book, for instance, at Lake Street Church, where distinctions between Christian and non-Christian truth

SIDEBAR C.2
Robert Wuthnow's Typology

In *America and the Challenges of Religious Diversity*, sociologist Robert Wuthnow proposes three categories based on data from his Religion and Diversity Survey: (1) *Spiritual shoppers* visit the religious marketplace for what they consider equally valid religious truth claims; (2) *Inclusivists* believe both that Christianity offers the best way to understand truth and that truth may also be found in other religions; (3) *Exclusivists* see truth as available only in Christianity and believe that non-Christians must convert to Christianity to be saved. The following graph shows the percentages of each category.

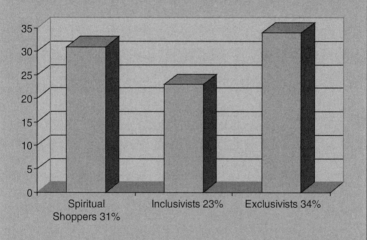

Source: Robert Wuthnow, *America and the Challenges of Religious Diversity* (Princeton, N.J.: Princeton University Press, 2005).

claims are barely acknowledged (chapter 6) and in New England Congregational Church's respectful recognition of the scriptures and teachings of other religions (chapter 11).

But what if we shift the focus away from religious truths claims and consideration of Christian doctrines? What happens when other issues take priority in interreligious relations?

Consider chapter 9, "Solidarity in the African American Experience: Churches and the Nation of Islam." There the primary issue was not religious truth claims but rather the powerful social realities of racism. Their shared minority status impelled African American Christians and Muslims to set aside doctrinal differences in order to collaborate on important community concerns. For the pastors featured in that chapter, a theology of the African American experience, not a calculus of doctrines, shapes their relationship with the Nation of Islam.

Recall also Rev. Larry Hodge (chapters 1 and 11). He and like-minded theological exclusivists in Aurora, Illinois, give no quarter to the religious truth claims of their non-Christian neighbors, but they differ from those Christian exclusivists who would ban all such idolaters from the United States. In fact, Rev. Hodge balanced his theological exclusivism with a kind of civic pluralism that grants Hindus, Muslims, and other non-Christians their constitutional right to pursue their false religious claims. For the good of the community, Rev. Hodge was willing to cooperate with spiritually benighted non-Christians and set aside his truth claim exclusivism in order to focus on other issues.

The friendship evangelism featured in chapters 2 and 3 also shifts the emphasis away from competing religious truth claims, though in a complex way. None of the evangelical Christians in either chapter would entertain the notion that other religions offer hope for eternal salvation. They are clear that the Christian Gospel must be spread throughout the non-Christian world, including among the non-Christian immigrants and refugees of the United States. Nonetheless, should evangelical strategy focus first on the truth claims of the Gospel or on the biblical mandate to show love to strangers and neighbors in need? Friendship evangelism employs the latter strategy and concentrates on the person first, the person's truth claims second. In practice, this means that truth claims may never be broached with some individuals, as we have heard from those who are quite content to leave the ultimate workings of salvation to the promptings of the Holy Spirit. Friendship evangelism has no truth claim strings attached to it, as Tom Williamson indicated (chapter 3). Friendship evangelists do not withdraw their friendship when those whom they befriend show no inclination to accept the Gospel message or even talk about it. Apparently, "Happy Hindu in the Bible Belt" (mentioned earlier) had not experienced this type of evangelism.

The Orthodox Christian experience featured in chapter 10 also speaks to this point about religious truth claims. No Christian group surpasses the Orthodox in their concern to protect the ancient truth of Christianity. Whether one labels them exclusivists or inclusivists, the Orthodox certainly are not pluralists. To them, Christianity is not one among many equally legitimate understandings of truth—witness the Orthodox delegation's withdrawal from the 1993 Parliament of the World's Religions mentioned in the introduction to this book. Yet the Orthodox encounter with Islam, in both the Old World and the United States, shifts the emphasis away from competing truth claims to that of dialogue and cooperation, a movement away from past conflicts and toward potential mutual redemption as peoples of a shared destiny.

Does this analysis suggest a useful classification of Christian perspectives on other religions? Some would argue that we already have enough typologies, all more or less useful in their own ways (see the resources listed at the end of the chapter under "For More Information"). Paul Knitter reminds us "that models are slippery. While they're useful for describing general approaches and attitudes, they almost never perfectly fit an individual theologian; they're fluid and often spill into each other."

Our analysis suggests that we should consider how Christians define "the other." Who or what is "the other" that local Christians perceive? If "the other" is competing religious truth claims, then typologies like exclusivism/inclusivism/pluralism can be useful. However, if "the other" is a neighbor in need, whether immigrants and refugees (chapter 3) or a Muslim group without a place to pray (chapter 4), or if "the other" represents a historical antagonist (chapter 10), then the otherness of their religious truth claims becomes a secondary consideration. The same holds for Christians who belong to a minority group threatened by an "other" that ignores distinctions of truth claims within the group. As Rev. James Demus noted (chapter 9), "Within the African American community, the issue is not the Nation of Islam versus Christianity, but religion versus the lure of the streets." For the Focolare Movement, the spirituality of "the other" creates a dialogue of love, an interfaith unity of kindred souls in the family of God that can transcend the diversity of religious truth claims (chapter 8).

To some extent, any identifiable group, religious or not, creates "otherness" simply by defining itself since boundaries distinguish "insiders" and "outsiders." Thus, by definition, Christians must face the other religious groups on America's changing landscape. One may draw a key distinction between Christians who focus on the others' truth claims and Christians who place different claims, such as human needs or social conditions, ahead of truth claims, at least for practical purposes. In either case, the main claim on Christians is that of understanding and living out their Christian calling in the face of the claims of others.

How Would All Christians Wish Others to Think of Them and the Christian Faith?

While writing this book, I was asked to preach at a congregation whose membership reflects two of the perspectives on religious diversity described in these chapters. Most of the members are immigrants whose forebears in India were converted from Hinduism and tribal religions by denominational missionaries. Many resonated with my description of the South Asian friendship evangelism of chapter 2, and after the service one person thanked me for giving him practical advice on how to approach his non-Christian acquaintances and extended family members. Others in the congregation, including the American-born generations of Indians and a few white members, resonated with their denomination's largely pluralist approach, which emphasizes interreligious dialogue.

I told everyone during that sermon that I did not care what perspective they adopt on other religions as long as they exhibit what I call "meek Christianity" in their dealings with the adherents of those religions. Most important to me is the attitude of meekness described throughout the New Testament.

The pertinent Greek word here, which appears sixteen times in the New Testament, carries a meaning of meekness, mildness,

gentleness, and humility. We find it in the Beatitude, "Blessed
are the *meek:* for they shall inherit the earth" (Matthew 5:5, King
James Version). It is used of Jesus on Palm Sunday, citing the
prophet Zechariah: "Look, your king is coming to you, *humble,*
and mounted on a donkey" (Matthew 21:5, New Revised Standard
Version). Jesus beckons: "Come to me, all who labor and are heavy
laden, and I will give you rest. Take my yoke upon you, and learn
from me; for I am *gentle* and lowly in heart, and you will find
rest for your souls. For my yoke is easy, and my burden is light"
(Matthew 11:28–30, Revised Standard Version).

The word appears several times in the Epistles. Paul entreats the
Christians in Corinth "By the *gentleness* and kindness of Christ"
(2 Corinthians 10:1, Today's English Version) and tells the
Colossians to "put on the garments that suit God's chosen people, his own, his beloved: compassion, kindness, humility, *gentleness,* patience" (Colossians 3:12, New English Bible). He implores
the Christians in Ephesus, "Be completely humble and *gentle;*
be patient, bearing with one another in love" (Ephesians 4:2,
New International Version). James writes, "If there are any wise
or learned men among you, let them show it by their good lives,
with *humility* and wisdom in their actions" (James 3:13, Jerusalem
Bible). In a passage with clear implications for interreligious
relations, 1 Peter says, "Always be ready to answer anyone who
demands of you an accounting of the hope that is yours. Yet [do
so] out of *humility* and reverence" (1 Peter 3:15–16, *Word Biblical
Commentary,* Word Books, Dallas).

Note the pairing of the two words *humility* and *reverence* in
this last passage. The Greek word translated here as "reverence"
is often rendered "respect" in English translations of the Bible.
Respect is a virtue in interreligious relations of any kind. It is the
first of four guiding principles in approaching other religions as
laid out by Asbury Seminary professor and prominent evangelical
scholar Terry C. Muck in his book *How to Study Religion:* "Respect
means not laughing at, mocking, or belittling the ideas that other
people use to order their lives." Muck clarifies that respect does
not necessitate agreement in all things: "Respecting other people's
beliefs doesn't mean indiscriminately agreeing with everything you
run across. However, it does entail realizing that these sometimes

strange beliefs are extremely important to people.... Civilized people do not belittle religious beliefs just because they are different. In a very important sense, as religious beings we are all in the same boat—searching for a safe harbor."

However, in talking about reverence, 1 Peter takes respect one step further for Christians. Our reverence before God makes us reverent among others. Reverence and humility intersect in characterizing the Christian life before God and neighbor. With regard to humility as a second guiding principle in approaching other religions, Terry Muck says:

> Human beings cannot fully fathom the extraordinary nature of God. This element of mystery, combined with our human status as creatures in the Creator-creature relationship, means that humility is the only proper response in the face of God's existence.... Humility is a way of doing a reality check. For Christians it means that even though we may think our religion is the one, true religion, we still don't know everything there is to know about God.

This offers a deep Christian foundation for civil discourse and charitable relations with adherents of other religions.

Christian meekness should not be confused with weakness. This meekness is spiritual strength, which can flow only when one empties oneself completely and fills the void with God's grace. The resulting attitude exudes divine love toward others, the kind of love Paul speaks about in the famous "love chapter" of 1 Corinthians, which he directed toward a church full of those who boasted about their spiritual gifts: "Love is patient; love is kind; love is not envious or boastful or arrogant or rude. It does not insist on its own way; it is not irritable or resentful; it does not rejoice in wrongdoing, but rejoices in the truth" (1 Corinthians 13:4–6, New Revised Standard Version).

Here is a reminder to Christians that truth comes from God and is a cause for rejoicing but never for boasting or arrogance. Whatever perspective a Christian adopts regarding adherents of other religions, it should include meekness of spirit. Consider the impression this will make in interreligious encounters.

For More Information

Diana L. Eck directs the Pluralism Project at Harvard University. In her spiritual autobiography, *Encountering God: A Spiritual Journey from Bozeman to Banaras* (Boston: Beacon Press, 1993), Eck outlines the exclusivism/inclusivism/pluralism typology and advocates Christian pluralism: "God always transcends what we humans can apprehend or understand. No tradition can claim the Holy or the Truth as its private property."

Gallup's Religious Tolerance Index is described by Albert L. Winseman, "Religious Tolerance Score Edged Up in 2004," http://www.gallup.com/poll/15253/Religious-Tolerance-Score-Edged-2004.aspx. Robert Wuthnow's *America and the Challenges of Religious Diversity* (Princeton, N.J.: Princeton University Press, 2005) provides an interesting and readable sociological analysis of Christian perspectives on America's new religious diversity. Wuthnow, a Presbyterian, advocates what he calls a "reflective pluralism" marked by serious and appreciative mutual inquiry about deeply held religious beliefs.

S. Mark Heim, *Grounds for Understanding: Ecumenical Resources for Responses to Religious Pluralism* (Grand Rapids, Mich.: Eerdmans, 1998), examines a wide range of Christian denominations and traditions and the various ways in which they conceive of the issues involved in facing religious diversity. Heim avoids typologies like exclusivism/inclusivism/pluralism and evangelism/dialogue as too simplistic to cover the great range of Christian approaches to other religions.

Paul F. Knitter, *Introducing Theologies of Religion* (Maryknoll, N.Y.: Orbis, 2002), offers a classification of replacement/fulfillment/mutuality/acceptance to describe how Christians have viewed Christianity's place among the world's religions. The publisher's blurb hails the book for "[a]voiding tired labels of past debates (Exclusivism, Pluralism, and Inclusivism)."

Terry C. Muck is a prolific evangelical Christian author and scholar of world religions. In *Those Other Religions in Your*

Neighborhood: Loving Your Neighbor When You Don't Know How (Grand Rapids, Mich.: Zondervan, 1992), Muck presents several typologies and identifies himself as a Christian exclusivist. He addresses what he calls "the challenge of non-Christian religions on American turf," which he sees as a matter of "religious competition." Each chapter answers a specific question about how Christians can speak the truth in love to their non-Christian neighbors. In *How to Study Religion* (Wilmore, Ky.: Wood Hill, 2005), Muck introduces the academic study of world religions to Christian students.

Don A. Pittman, Ruben L. F. Habito, and Terry C. Muck, eds., *Ministry and Theology in Global Perspective: Contemporary Challenges for the Church* (Grand Rapids, Mich.: Eerdmans, 1996) covers the topics of a Christian theology of other religions, Christian missions, and interreligious dialogue from a Christian perspective. The book provides useful overviews of various Christian approaches to other religions, including summaries of exclusivism, inclusivism, and pluralism.

Alan Race, *Christians and Religious Pluralism: Patterns in the Christian Theology of Religions* (London: SCM, 1983), provides a detailed and critical analysis of the exclusivism/inclusivism/pluralism typology. Race identifies himself as a Christian pluralist: "I have defended this approach as the most positive Christian response to the encounter between Christianity and the world faiths."

Owen C. Thomas offers a complex typological discussion in *Attitudes toward Other Religions: Some Christian Interpretations* (New York: Harper & Row, 1969).

For Discussion

1. Evaluate the typologies of Christian perspectives on other religions described in this chapter. How useful are they, particularly the well-known exclusivism/inclusivism/pluralism classification? Do they explain all of the case studies presented in this book? Do they

illuminate your own experiences of Christians interacting with non-Christians? Can you propose a more useful typology?

2. Discuss the distinction between a focus on truth claims and a focus on other claims. How important are Christianity's truth claims to you and your congregation? Do you consider them the highest priority in interreligious encounters? If not, what takes higher priority in your mind?

3. Explore the implications of the "meek Christianity" attitude. Can all Christians, regardless of their perspectives on other religions, agree to adopt this attitude in interreligious encounters? How will non-Christians respond to such an attitude? Which individuals or groups in this book best modeled this attitude in their approach to other religions?

4. Now that you have finished this book, what will you and your congregation do about the religious diversity in your area? Remember: You do not have the option of doing "nothing" since even avoidance is doing something.

5. Bible passages: This chapter has already cited half of the sixteen New Testament occurrences of the Greek word that underlies the "meek Christianity" attitude. Here are the other eight occurrences: 1 Corinthians 4:21; Galatians 5:22–23; Galatians 6:1; 1 Timothy 6:11; 2 Timothy 2:24–25; Titus 3:2; James 1:21; 1 Peter 3:4.

Index